THE SCHOOL OF NIGHT

THE SCHOOL OF NIGHT

by Peter Whelan

WARNER CHAPPELL PLAYS

LONDON

A Time Warner Company

First published in 1992
by Warner Chappell Plays Ltd
129 Park Street, London W1Y 3FA

Reprinted 1993

ISBN 0 85676 159 1

Printed by Commercial Colour Press, London E7

THE SCHOOL OF NIGHT was first performed by the Royal Shakespeare Company at The Other Place, Stratford Upon Avon, on 4th November, 1992, and was produced by arrangement with Mike Merrick and Edward Rissen. The cast was as follows:

CHRISTOPHER MARLOWE	Richard McCabe
THOMAS KYD	Adrian Lukis
INGRAM FRIZER	Graham Turner
TOM STONE	Nigel Cooke
THOMAS WALSINGHAM	John McAndrew
ROSALINDA BENOTTI	Bella Enahoro
AUDRY WALSINGHAM	Rebecca Saire
SIR WALTER RALEGH	Jack Klaff
ROBYN POLEY	Antony Bunsee
NICHOLAS SKERES	Lloyd Hutchinson
AN OFFICER OF THE WATCH	Ken Christensen

QUEENS OFFICERS, COMMEDIA ACTORS

Directed by Bill Alexander
Designed by Fotini Dimou
Lighting by Brian Harris
Music by Ilona Sekacz

CAST OF CHARACTERS

CHRISTOPHER MARLOWE	Late twenties
TOM STONE	Late twenties
THOMAS WALSINGHAM	Late twenties
AUDRY WALSINGHAM	Mid twenties
ROSALINDA BENOTTI	A Moor, early twenties
THOMAS KYD	Early thirties
SIR WALTER RALEGH	Late thirties
INGRAM FRIZER	Mid thirties
ROBYN POLEY	Thirties
NICHOLAS SKERES	Thirties

To be doubled:

QUEEN'S OFFICERS
COMMEDIA ACTORS
AN OFFICER OF THE WATCH

The action takes place between Summer 1592 and Spring 1593.

THE SCHOOL OF NIGHT was inspired by the works of Calvin Hoffman.

ACT ONE

Scene One

Scadbury, Kent. A room in TOM WALSINGHAM'S *country house, turned by* MARLOWE *into a study-library and 'alchemist's cell', with star charts, astrolabe, globe, maps, cabalistic signs and glass retorts. A stuffed alligator hangs from the ceiling.*

Touches of Venice and the Orient, as seen in lamps, silks and ornaments, contrast with the room's sturdy Tudor style.

It is almost dawn. MARLOWE *has worked through the night. Now he offers up a 'prayer' with a mixture of bitterness, mockery and intense seriousness.*

MARLOWE   Immortal, invisible, all-seeing, all-smelling, brown-eyed, wet-nosed Dog! Let me have knowledge and see the future. Almighty Dog, who hast brought me to the beginning of this day, be with me now, protect me with thy mighty paw. Let fall on me thy canine salivation! Eternal Dog! Scratch the path my feet must follow and sniff me out the man I am to become! Through Jesus Cur, born of the blessed Virgin Bitch. In the name of Dog the Sire, Dog the Whelp and Dog the Holy Hound!

     (*Silence. He concentrates, trying to raise a vision in his mind.*)

     Show me. Show me the vision as I saw it before. The room. The silent figures. The river beyond.

     (*Nothing. His mocking tone returns.*)

     I ask you for knowledge, Dog, because that other Deity who would usurp thy Doghead and spelleth thy name backwards, keeps it from me! Nor will the Devil enlighten me or come to me at my command.

(*He opens a great book and recites from Faustus.*)

"Orientis princeps Belzebub inferni ardentis monarcha et Demogorgon propitiamus vos ut appareat et surgat Mephistophilis!"

(*He waits mockingly. Silence.*)

You see what I mean? I have cast doubts upon the existence of the immortal soul, so I have nothing to bargain with. O, I will leap up to my Dog! Who pulls me down?

(*A cock crows. The coincidence amuses him.*)

Do you deny me?

(*It crows again.*)

Thrice?

(*Silence. He lies on a settle. The light from the windows is eerily phosphorescent. He concentrates.*)

MARLOWE   I smell water . . . Yes! I smell the river! Show me. Show me my future.

(*A humming note. The light increases, ghostly white and the room is transformed into another room of his imagination. It is an austere white room, small, and full of the reflected light of a river outside the window. It contains a bench and table upstage. Three men, muffled up in cloaks and hats sit at the table with their backs to us. MARLOWE still lies downstage, his back towards them.*)

[*During the transformation we hear formal courtly music as though this might be a transformation scene in a masque.*]

The room. Three men who don't turn to see me nor I to see them. Three silent motionless figures. I can't look at them. But I can question. Gentlemen . . . good morning. I believe you have come to tell me, not of my death . . . but of some new possibility in my life. Of some change in my being . . . a new power to lift me far beyond what I am now . . . a new science that will give me wings to fly as effortlessly as this river light laps the walls of this room. Tell me. Who am I to become?

(*The light begins to fade.*)

I'll hold you! I'll make you answer! It always begins with the smell of water and if I keep the smell of water I can hold you!

(*He takes a deep breath. The scene fades and we are back in the library at Scadbury . . . but now in the clear light of a summer morning. The three men have turned, revealing themselves as* TOM KYD, INGRAM FRIZER *and* TOM STONE, *all having just dismounted outside and walked straight into the room.* STONE *is tense at the prospect of meeting* MARLOWE *for the first time.* MARLOWE *seems at first to be asleep.*)

KYD   Good morning Kit! Here's your actor.

(*He pulls up short and motions the other two to be quiet. He creeps across the room but suddenly* MARLOWE *wakes with a cry belonging to his vision.*)

MARLOWE   Answer me! I'll hold you . . . answer me!

KYD   Answer you what?

(MARLOWE *turns, can't take them in.*)

MARLOWE   Tom? Ingram? Who's this?

KYD

The trouble with you is you never sleep at the right times.

MARLOWE

No . . . I was awake. Wide awake.

(*He says this in reference to the vision he saw. The effect disturbs the others.*)

FRIZER

This is Thomas Stone, Master Marlowe. You wanted an actor . . .

KYD

You asked Ingram to find you one yesterday . . . while he was in Chislehurst.

(KYD *stares silently at* STONE.)

FRIZER

His company have been touring around Kent. But they disbanded last week, so he was happy to take up your invitation and come to Scadbury.

KYD

You're lucky he's free.

MARLOWE

Master Stone . . .

STONE

I'm very proud to meet you.

MARLOWE

I imagine you've performed in a country house before?

STONE

Yes.

MARLOWE

You'll be the guest of the owner, Master Thomas Walsingham . . . as I am. Have they told you what's wanted?

STONE

A quick learner.

MARLOWE

You'll only have to do one scene. From *Dido, Queen of Carthage*. You won't know the play. I've never had it done in public.

STONE

For tonight?

MARLOWE	I'm not looking for the performance of a life-time. Master Walsingham has an important visitor arriving. This is the entertainment. You're Aeneas . . . son of Venus.

(*He looks at* STONE, *dubiously.*)

STONE	He's disappointed.
KYD	Nonsense . . .
STONE	I said you would be.
MARLOWE	No . . . just older than I expected.
FRIZER	He's the same age as you!
MARLOWE	Is he? Well . . . I'm older than I expected. So . . . your company's disbanded. How's Gwillam?

(MARLOWE *is 'testing'.* STONE *realises it.*)

He still runs the company, doesn't he?

STONE	Yes. It's broken his heart. He's forced to sell the costumes.
MARLOWE	What did you play?
STONE	Kings, Senators, Hermits . . . the Pope.
MARLOWE	In *Faustus*? On tour?
STONE	No, in London. At the Rose . . . twice only.

(MARLOWE *seems to doubt this slightly.*)

KYD	The Rose? You weren't in one of mine, were you? (*Sees that* STONE *does not know him.*) Tom Kyd . . .
STONE	*The Spanish Tragedy* . . . no.

MARLOWE	Just *Faustus*?
STONE	Yes.
MARLOWE	Good. We'll possibly do a scene from *Faustus*. But Dido's the main thing.

(STONE *sways slightly.* MARLOWE *is alarmed.*)

What's the matter?

STONE	I'm sorry. I didn't have time for a meal this morning.

(MARLOWE *moves away from him.*)

MARLOWE	When was he last in London?
STONE	Two months ago.
MARLOWE	Are you sure?
FRIZER	Knowing you, d'you think I'd be such a fool?
KYD	What d'you want to do? Inspect his crotch and armpits?
MARLOWE	Why not?
KYD	England's Merlin afraid? Where are your magic powers?
STONE	I've no infection, sir. •

(*Suddenly he strips off his doublet and shirt and lifts his arms.*)

MARLOWE	Oh sir! I've insulted you. Here! (*He strips off his doublet.*) Now we're equal. Now we're the same.

(KYD *exchanges a glance with* FRIZER.)

KYD	Perhaps we'd better leave.

MARLOWE   We'll spare you the rest . . . you having been
            so recently in the saddle. There's bread, a
            dish of eggs and strawberries.

            (*He offers food.* STONE *has put his clothes
            back on.*)

            No more doubts on my side. Let's see if you
            have any on yours. Welcome to Scadbury.
            You'll meet your host, Tom Walsingham, and
            his wife, Mistress Audry. A powerful family.
            His late cousin, Sir Francis, secretary to the
            Privy Council. So, all in all, very close
            connections with *herself* . . .

            (*He pulls himself up.*)

            Ingram . . . those musicians . . . d'you mind?

FRIZER   I'll get them.

            (*He exits, well aware that he is excluded,
            giving them a little smile.* MARLOWE *addresses*
            STONE.)

MARLOWE   What d'you make of Ingram?

STONE   He seems very clear-minded. Precise.

MARLOWE   Never met him before?

STONE   No.

KYD   He's a spy. They're all spies here. And I mean
            "spies" . . . not your common or garden
            informers. Even Kit's one.

            (MARLOWE *is not pleased by this.*)

MARLOWE   Ingram's a professional. I've played at it . . .
            "But that was in another country . . ."

(STONE *smiles, recognising the quotation from*
"The Jew of Malta".)

STONE   ". . . and besides the wench is dead."

MARLOWE   D'you know who it is you're here to
             entertain?

KYD   He doesn't.

             (*Again*, MARLOWE *shows an edge of irritation.*
             STONE *notices it.*)

STONE   No. I don't.

MARLOWE   But you'll have guessed at his importance.

STONE   His?

             (MARLOWE *and* KYD *are amused.*)

MARLOWE   It's not *her*.

KYD   The Queen? No, not Her Majesty. You'd have
             never got within five miles of the house if it
             had been.

MARLOWE   All the same, very close to her.

             (*He leaves a silence.*)

STONE   The Earl of Essex?

MARLOWE   No. Not the noble earl. Too high.

KYD   Try the other . . .

STONE   Other?

KYD   Favourite.

STONE   Her Spaniard?

             (MARLOWE *looks at him sharply.*)

Sir Walter Ralegh?

MARLOWE   Yes. You're well informed. 'Spaniard'?

STONE   His nickname. Because of his swarthy
               appearance.

MARLOWE   Who told you that?

STONE   I thought it was common knowledge.

KYD   Not outside court circles.

(*A pause while they let this pass.*)

MARLOWE   Yes, you're right. Sir Walter. He's a generous
               man but a dangerous one. Now that there are
               signs of a fracture in her favouritism . . .

(*He notes* STONE'S *surprise.*)

               Oh yes . . . he could be even more dangerous
               . . . in not knowing who his real friends are.
               Tonight I want him to face the truth about
               himself. He was my friend. A poet. A man of
               action, enlightenment, knowledge. And such
               is the state we live in that this man is reduced
               to pretending love to one Royal and Ancient
               Virgin. Well Tom? Is the whole world
               suddenly called Tom? You, as our guest will
               be Tom . . . Kyd will be Thom-*arse*.

(MARLOWE *laughs suggestively.*)

KYD   Marlowe's wit. Impenetrable.

MARLOWE   Tom Walsingham we will call "Tam" because
               of certain Scottish expectations he and his
               wife secretly entertain . . .

KYD   ⎫   (*falsetto and very Scots*) Lang live Queen
MARLOWE ⎭   James!

MARLOWE   So. Tom. One final question. You're a
           Protestant?

STONE   Of course . . .

MARLOWE   Of course. How strong is your protest?

STONE   As strong as Her Majesty and the Archbishop
           require.

           (MARLOWE *is impressed by the diplomatic
           reply.*)

MARLOWE   Walter Ralegh was once associated with
           myself and others in a society for the pursuit
           of learning. All kinds of learning . . . as we
           shall remind him. Assuming you agree to take
           part you must also decide whether to read
           this . . .

KYD   (*sharply*) Kit . . .

           (MARLOWE *hands* STONE *a paper.* STONE *reads
           carefully.*)

MARLOWE   It is blasphemy, sir . . . but only to be uttered
           amongst consenting adults.

STONE   You intend "Dog" - to stand for the deity?

MARLOWE   Oh no. Dog is entirely different. He's my
           deity. A most amenable and friendly deity.
           The kind of deity you can be on all fours
           with.

STONE   How d'you want it?

           (*Again,* MARLOWE *is impressed by* STONE'S
           *cool manner . . . but a touch suspicious. Is
           the man too ready to agree?* STONE *reads this
           thought.*)

           When I've decided.

MARLOWE   In the tone that most pleases Almighty Dog . . .

                (*Suddenly he throws back his head and howls.*
                KYD *stays out of it.* STONE *observes, a little
                smile on his lips. He is calculating the
                moment to go along with this. He begins to
                bark. The doors are opened and* TOM
                WALSINGHAM *enters, bearing a staff which he
                strikes on the floor in a major domo manner.*)

WALSINGHAM   Silence! Her Majesty the Queen!

                (*Music strikes up in the next room. Enter*
                ROSALINDA, *the Moor, shimmering and regal in
                her Queen Dido costume.* STONE *is amazed.*
                AUDRY WALSINGHAM *follows as a lady in
                waiting.*)

ROSALINDA   "What stranger art thou that dost eye me
                thus?"

                (*This 'skit' on the meeting of Dido and
                Aeneas is more intended as a joke on*
                MARLOWE . . . *not without a sharp edge to it,
                especially from* AUDRY.)

WALSINGHAM   "Sometime he was a Trojan, mighty Queen;
                But Troy is not - what shall I say he is?"

AUDRY   "Renowned Dido, 'tis our General, warlike
                Aeneas."

ROSALINDA   "Warlike Aeneas, and in these base robes!"

MARLOWE   You finished? Tom Stone. This is your Dido.

ROSALINDA   I have a name.

MARLOWE   Rosalinda Benotti. "The Leopardess."

ROSALINDA   "Brave prince, welcome to Carthage and to
                me."

KYD   Kit loves surprises.

ROSALINDA   Are you surprised?

STONE   Very.

WALSINGHAM   Master Stone . . .

                 (*For a minute* STONE *thinks he is an actor he
                 may have met.*)

STONE   Ah . . .

MARLOWE   No you have not worked together; he is not,
                 as you may have guessed, an actor - he is your
                 genial host Master Thomas Walsingham,
                 aided and abetted, surprisingly, by Mistress
                 Audry Walsingham. Nothing here is as it
                 seems.

WALSINGHAM   Forgive us. We were looking through Kit's
                 play that you are to perform and . . . we were
                 suddenly amused by the appropriateness of
                 the lines to your arrival here.

MARLOWE   Welcome to Scadbury.

WALSINGHAM   Welcome.

STONE   I thank you sir . . . madam.

                 (*He bows to her gracefully.*)

AUDRY   Your actor is quite the courtier . . .

STONE   We are well coached madam.

AUDRY   You must miss London . . .

                 (*Before he can reply she suddenly utters a
                 prayer, testing to detect his orthodoxy.*)

                 Almighty God deliver our sovereign Queen
                 and her devoted subjects from this present
                 pestilence. Amen.

(WALSINGHAM, KYD *and* ROSALINDA *say their
'amens' . . .* STONE *is a beat too late.*)

MARLOWE   He needs rehearsal.

WALSINGHAM   I look forward to your performance.

STONE   So would I, sir, if I knew more properly what
               it was.

WALSINGHAM   Don't let him spring too many surprises.

AUDRY   You're a brave prince indeed to travel about
               in these times. Especially in Kent.

ROSALINDA   I've seen you. Where have I seen him?

MARLOWE   (*interested*) The Rose Theatre?

STONE   I only played in two performances. Mostly
               I've toured.

ROSALINDA   No . . . not the Rose. But it was in London.

AUDRY   You know one of your company's been
               arrested?

               (FRIZER *has entered.*)

FRIZER   Name of Abel Mossman?

STONE   Abel Mossman . . . he was our clown. What
               charge?

FRIZER   Catholic agent. Another invasion scare.
               They're stopping everything that moves
               between here and Dover.

AUDRY   (*observing the effect keenly*) They say he was
               carrying a portrait of the Madonna behind a
               miniature portrait of his wife.

FRIZER	Also a Catholic crucifix in the heel of his shoe.

ROSALINDA   *Meschinità!* They have nothing better to do!

MARLOWE   I sometimes think the Queen's officers spend half their time destroying footwear!

STONE   Where is he now?

FRIZER   Maidstone. For a few pressing questions.

(WALSINGHAM *speaks carefully, making his position clear.*)

WALSINGHAM   It must distress you that one of your number should lapse in this way.

STONE   I wish I could help . . . (*He stops himself saying 'him'.*)

AUDRY   Help?

(MARLOWE *is quick to 'rescue' him.*)

MARLOWE   You can help . . . by learning Aeneas quickly. And acting him tellingly, hmmm? Rehearse him Rosalinda. We'll leave them to it and hear the musicians. You must all assist me in choosing the music.

AUDRY   Assist a genius? There's a task!

(*All exit except* ROSALINDA *and* STONE.)

ROSALINDA   I'm sorry for your friend, the clown.

STONE   He wasn't a friend. I disliked him heartily. I couldn't stand his jokes. Poor Mossman.

ROSALINDA   So we're to act together. Am I a surprise?

STONE   Yes.

ROSALINDA   Well, I suppose you were expecting a boy.
                   Some little pimple-face. In Italy we have
                   women playing women. Real women - not
                   pervertiti.

STONE   You're Italian?

ROSALINDA   Venice. You know the Commedia? Commedia
                   dell Arte? That's *real* theatre. You have
                   nothing like it in England.

                   (STONE *nods.*)

ROSALINDA   My father played Pantalone, the old miser. He
                   was famous in the Commedia. My mother
                   was the funny maid, you know? She was a
                   dancer. A slave. She served in the court in
                   Morocco. My father bought her. Married her.
                   The troupe comes to London and father gets
                   the plague. The others go on and mother and I
                   stay to nurse him. But the Queen of Heaven
                   loved him too much. (*She makes a small sign
                   of the cross, a forbidden gesture.*) Then we
                   found the plague had gone from him to my
                   mother . . . I became a beggar . . . dancing
                   outside the theatres. Oh people came from
                   everywhere to see me. I think I could have
                   been rich . . . until the disease closed all the
                   theatres and I was on my way to the devil. Kit
                   heard about it. He hasn't much use for a
                   woman . . . you know? But he took me and
                   made me his pet leopardess. When the
                   theatres open again he has promised me
                   Zenocrete in *Tamburlaine*! *Bando alle
                   chiacchierre!* [Let's get back to the subject.]

                   (STONE *notes the feeling of bitterness. She
                   hands him a manuscript.*)

                   D'you know *Dido Queen of Carthage*?

STONE   It's the only one of his plays I don't know.

ROSALINDA	It's - *perverso* - perverted. A scurvy play! Scurvy! Whoreson! It has Jupiter and the pretty boy Ganymede . . . what is it? Dallying! Kit says: "It is not for the million".

(She sizes him up.)

Did we meet? In London?

STONE	I can't be sure.

(She feels that he knows they did and is disguising it in his answer.)

ROSALINDA	But if we did . . . you wouldn't forget me . . . surely?

(STONE *smiles and agrees. Music from the other room. Fade lights.*)

Scene Two

The same, that evening. AUDRY *and* WALSINGHAM *discovered.*

AUDRY	He shouldn't be here! He shouldn't set foot in this house.
WALSINGHAM	Walter Ralegh is an old friend. It's an informal, friendly visit.
AUDRY	He should have no friends!
WALSINGHAM	This is churlish. I heard he was at Chatham disbanding the fleet and merely suggested he should break his journey on his way back to London.
AUDRY	When the Queen withdraws her favour she expects us to do the same!
WALSINGHAM	There you misread her. She approves this visit because, secretly, she wants to know Ralegh's mind and trusts us to tell her. He only comes

here because he wants to know her mind . . .
and hopes we'll tell him.

AUDRY   My father warned you: have nothing to do
                 with Ralegh.

WALSINGHAM   I hear his warning and will respond in my
                 own way . . . he's coming!

                 (RALEGH and FRIZER enter and they take up
                 tobacco pipes.)

RALEGH   Tom! Audry! I was just telling Ingram about
                 my man Hariot's account of his voyage to the
                 new world . . . He said that where they first
                 landed the coast was low and sandy right
                 down to the water's edge, but so filled with
                 grapes that the very beating and surge of the
                 sea o'erflowed them. It presented me such a
                 picture of the abundance of the Americas that
                 I laughed out loud. Vines grew in every shrub,
                 he said, and even climbed to the tops of high
                 cedars and more fruitful than any in France or
                 Italy. And they met the people there . . . they
                 were dressed simply in animal skins . . . yet
                 the women resembling, in figure and face,
                 ladies of rank and fashion they had seen in
                 England! Well these American people, it
                 seems, are as mannerly and civilised as any in
                 Europe.

WALSINGHAM   And she called it Virginia?

RALEGH   Her name, yes. Virginia. Sweet Virgin Queen,
                 it was all for thee! To see my ships return that
                 I might lay those riches at your feet.

WALSINGHAM   She has a good nose for investment.

                 (RALEGH is stung by this.)

                 I mean in capability. In yourself, Sir Walter.
                 Your expeditions.

(RALEGH *holds on to the fit of pique then
suddenly laughs heartily. There is a hint of
danger in his nervous state.*)

RALEGH   You're right! She's shrewd! "When are you
going to stop begging?" she asks . . . if I've
offered some good means of profit for the
crown that requires a thousand or two on the
table . . . "When you stop giving", I say . . .
keeping up the pretence I'm asking for a gift,
you know, that's the way we have to do these
transactions. She lifts her little finger . . .
such a little, little finger and practically uses
it as a pen to write what she says next:
"You'll find our self may not always be so
generous." Ah . . . yes.

(*A slight bleak silence as the Queen's remark
sinks in on* RALEGH.)

I freely admit I owe everything to her
largesse. It's as those who wish to smear me
say: ten years ago I could only afford one
servant. Now I could keep five hundred.

AUDRY   And most of them with you judging by the
state of our hall.

RALEGH   (*laughs*) My poor Devon lads . . . shattered by
the Panamanian fiasco. They're seamen I'm
helping to their homes. We must be sure
Rogers leaves you four horseloads of
provisions I earmarked for you Tom . . . no
argument! All to be disposed of now. And, of
course, it's not *her* doing. It's not her fault
that the entire expedition to Panama got no
further than Chatham! Look at her advisers!
Look at the Privy Council. Robert Cecil! No
fool . . . but never got a foot wet in his life
. . . and he can advise on ships, whether we
sail . . . where we sail! Her little manikin.
Queen's monkey! And then there's Sir
Christopher Hatton and other nameless ones

who poison her mind against me. Poison her mind . . .

(*He senses that he is beginning to become tedious on the subject and changes tone.*)

As I was once held to be poisoning her with that! (*The tobacco.*)

AUDRY	By the way . . . I think it's cured my back pains.
RALEGH	I told you. Clears all the bodily passages!
WALSINGHAM	I thought it might cure a cold.
RALEGH	Didn't it?
WALSINGHAM	No.
RALEGH	Pity. (*He suddenly shudders.*) Tom . . . Audry . . . tell me what goes on. Why doesn't she reply to my letters?
AUDRY	She can't have received them.
RALEGH	Chatham to Greenwich? No . . . no . . . I know what you mean. Her monkey manikin Cecil keeps them from her. Audry . . . don't spare me . . . does she banish me from conversation?
AUDRY	I remember her saying if you were going to be away so much she would have a horse called Sir Walter . . . so he might be under her and she on top and that was like to give the greatest pleasure!

(RALEGH *roars with - slightly forced - laughter.*)

RALEGH	Oh how she teases me! And she could ride me like Alexander . . . just as she hunts like Diana walks like Venus . . . the gentle wind blowing her fair hair about her pure cheeks, like a nymph . . . sometime sitting in the

shade like a Goddess, sometime singing like
an angel; sometime playing like Orpheus as
the lamps are lit. I think I love her most of all
by candlelight . . . blazing with jewels in the
dark . . . her eyes looking straight at you like
drawn swords.

(*We hear the musicians tuning up in the next
room.*)

WALSINGHAM   Merlin is at hand.

RALEGH   Ah Kit! Sweet Kit. Or is he sour . . . more
like?

AUDRY   Wait and see . . .

(RALEGH *laughs at* MARLOWE's *library.*)

RALEGH   All these books! *Principles of Alchemy*?
What's he trying to do here? Turn lead to
gold?

(FRIZER *has opened the door, having made
sure that* MARLOWE *is ready. He makes a fine
entrance in his 'Merlin' robe. Applause.*
ROSALINDA, KYD *and* STONE *will peep round
the door and make their entrance watching
'the show'.*)

MARLOWE   "Come live with me and be my love
And we will all the pleasures prove
That hills and valleys, dales and fields,
Woods, or steepy mountain yields."

RALEGH   (*quoting his own 'answer poem'*)
"If all the world and love were young,
And truth in every shepherd's tongue,
These pretty pleasures might me move,
To live with thee and be they love!"

My Merlin! To see you hold court again in
such a fair house designed for summer and

study and retreat. Have you space for your fellow poet and philosopher?

MARLOWE   Why? Are you quitting the court?

(RALEGH *makes a joke of it and hands him his pipe.*)

RALEGH   Here, sorcerer. I remember you saying when my man Hariot brought home tobacco from Roanoke that he who loves it not is a fool.

MARLOWE   What I actually said was: "He who loves not tobacco *and boys* . . . is a fool."

(RALEGH *dislikes this attempt to include him as a fellow homosexual.* WALSINGHAM *rescues him.*)

WALSINGHAM   Ah! Then, after all, Sir Walter, you are only half foolish.

(RALEGH *recovers his nervy good humour.*)

RALEGH   I think it would be generally accepted that love of *women* was my undoing. Speaking of which . . .

(*He sees* ROSALINDA. *Kisses her.*)

My Africa! You're playing the Queen of Carthage . . . of course! Carthage is in Africa! Therefore . . .

ROSALINDA   Dido was an African! And so are you. All of you! All Africans . . .

RALEGH   How?

ROSALINDA   Europa who rode on Zeus' back to Crete founded the European race . . . but she, too, came from Carthage. Europa was an African. Just think! All Europeans are descended from an African!

WALSINGHAM   Then why are we so pale?

ROSALINDA   With yearning for the sun.

              (RALEGH *kneels to her, in mock solemnity.*)

RALEGH   Then, ancestral queen, I kneel to you as I will
              kneel tomorrow to my beloved, radiant
              Angelica, my royal mistress . . . and ask her
              forgiveness.

ROSALINDA   Why? What have you done?

              (*An embarrassed silence.*)

MARLOWE   Walter. You're holding up Aeneas, played by
              Master Thomas Stone . . .

              (MARLOWE *looks for any sign of recognition.*)

RALEGH   Forgive me . . . good evening sir . . . and?

KYD   (*annoyed at not being introduced*) Tom Kyd.

RALEGH   Two of the muses' darlings under one roof!

KYD   You mean yourself and Kit.

RALEGH   You sir! I saw your play *The Spanish
              Tragedy*. When your Heironimo bit out his
              tongue, rather than be questioned, I said here
              is a man who knows the spirit of our times!
              Now . . . I take it, this entertainment is to be
              equally revealing . . . Tom?

WALSINGHAM   My intelligence does not stretch so far.

RALEGH   Audry?

AUDRY   My attention is rather taken with the real
              world, Sir Walter . . . not with 'shows'.

(*He takes his seat.* KYD *wheels in a lamp constructed in a wooden frame containing lenses and mirrors.*)

MARLOWE First the engine designed for us by your servant Hariot, that increases the brilliance of light by use of lenses and mirrors though the light source itself is not increased.

(*Applause for the effect.*)

RALEGH What an age of science we live in!

MARLOWE Prologue. This is presented by the mother of Aeneas, Venus . . .

AUDRY Which I refused to play . . .

MARLOWE And so . . . since Kyd hadn't the figure . . .

(*Blackout. Lights rise, and* MARLOWE *appears as Boticelli's Venus, with a flowing wig held to his crotch. With a painted shell behind him,* MARLOWE *looks strangely compelling, even beautiful.*)

AUDRY Another of Kit's surprises . . .

FRIZER Shall I bring some light?

WALSINGHAM That, I'm sure, is what Kit intends to do . . .

MARLOWE The story is that Aeneas, after the sack of Troy, sails the seas on his ill-fated Panamanian expedition . . .

(RALEGH *joins in the laughter.*)

Or rather . . . attempts to sail to Italy but is wrecked on the shores of Africa . . . lacking your navigational skill . . . There, in a sea cave, he meets with *his* Angelica, his Dido, his queen.

(Kyd, *operating the lamp, produces a beautiful effect.* Rosalinda *and* Stone *appear, searching for each other.*)

ROSALINDA   Aeneas!

STONE   Dido!

ROSALINDA   "Tell me, dear love, how found you out this cave?"

STONE   "By chance, sweet Queen, as Mars and Venus met."

ROSALINDA   "But that was in a net . . . where we are loose; And yet I am not free . . . Oh would I were!"

STONE   "Why . . . what is it that Dido may desire?"

ROSALINDA   "Aeneas, O Aeneas, quench these flames!"

(Stone *changes the tone, giving it more bite, a subtle satirising of* Ralegh's *relationship with Queen Elizabeth I.*)

STONE   "If that your majesty can look so low
As my despised worths that shun all praise
With this, my hand, I give to you my heart
And vow, by all the Gods of hospitality
Whiles Dido lives and rules in Juno's town,
Never to like or love any but her!"

(*He kneels in a mockery of* Ralegh *kneeling previously.* Ralegh, *still trying to control himself, stands abruptly.*)

RALEGH   Who is that actor?

WALSINGHAM   You go too far Kit!

RALEGH   How does he go too far, Tom? Tell me. Audry? Ingram . . . you must know. We'll ask your servants. Fetch the ostler and the scullery maid! In a nest of spies like this, who wouldn't know? And how far through the network has the message gone? How far through the country? Well, if it's an open secret let's be open. Mistress Audry, what are they saying?

AUDRY   That the Queen's Captain of the Guard has been unfaithful to his royal mistress . . . by getting one of her ladies in waiting with child and covertly marrying without Her Majesty's permission . . . which is an act of treason.

RALEGH   (*appealing to* ROSALINDA) Africa! Dear Africa . . . I couldn't bring myself to tell her I'd deceived her. Now she knows. Doesn't she, Ingram?

FRIZER   Yes.

RALEGH   And makes herself cold towards me. And bides her time. Without her I'm nothing but a bare gentleman. I've nothing she can't take.

MARLOWE   She can't take your mind.

RALEGH   She's taken my heart.

MARLOWE   That's all pretence! Face the truth. There is a realm of poetry and a realm of power. You can't live in both! Poets must always stand against the powerful or truth would die. I want us to reconvene the School of Night . . .

RALEGH   Of night? Ah! Of 'Knight'. I am a knight . . . is it a school of chivalry? Am I to go there for instruction?

MARLOWE   I'm asking you to pursue knowledge with me as you once did.

RALEGH   She is the fountainhead of knowledge . . .

MARLOWE   Only the knowledge the church allows!

RALEGH   Be careful, Kit . . . be very careful . . .

MARLOWE   Who once argued that the soul didn't exist?

AUDRY   No! I won't listen!

RALEGH   I never argued that the soul didn't exist! I
                merely enquired where it might be found.

MARLOWE   Who once disputed with me, from sunset to
                first light, that religion was only invented to
                keep the people in awe and subjection?

RALEGH   Why must you offend against your Creator?

MARLOWE   My Creator? Surely He didn't create me?
                Creatures of my sort? Shall we dispute that?

                (*Silence. Then* RALEGH *turns to* ROSALINDA,
                KYD *and* STONE.)

RALEGH   Thank you for the entertainment. More would
                be superfluous.

KYD   I'm sorry for the part I took. It was wrong!
                Totally wrong!

                (MARLOWE *gives* KYD *a look of utter contempt.*
                ROSALINDA, KYD *and* STONE *exit.*)

RALEGH   Mistress Audry. It would be a great favour if
                some supper were set for me in the hall.

                (*She curtsies and exits.* RALEGH *draws the
                dagger from the back of his belt.*)

RALEGH   Is this what you want, Kit? To see the iron
                walking? If you want it . . . it will! Who are
                you with? Them? Are you their trap-maker?
                You ask me to face the truth. I face it! She
                gave me life. Built me up. Raised the tower
                from which I see the world. I'm hers!

(*He turns and walks towards* WALSINGHAM *and* FRIZER. *As all three have their backs turned the room is suddenly transformed into the one in Kit's vision . . . the same watery light, the same sounds.* MARLOWE *turns towards the audience. Sounds of a river.*)

I had a friend once whose thirst for truth raged like mine. But he became the Queen's Captain of the Guard. Now she has a new nickname for him. "Water." "Sir Water." And his thirst rages no more.

(*The lights fade.*)

Scene Three

The same, the next morning. STONE, *avoiding* RALEGH *who will be breakfasting in the hall, eats and drinks various things he has brought in.* KYD *packs some books and belongings to take to London.*

KYD   I only came here for money. Money! I've lost almost everything through Kit. My patron cut me off when he heard I'd once shared a room with him. A certain nobleman who shall be nameless now pretends I don't exist because I'd been associated with the arch-atheist.

STONE   Have some breakfast. They've gone from the hall. They'll be saddling up. Here, these are good.

             (KYD *takes a small cake or two.*)

             They know how to choose a cook. I shall eat while I can. I feel lean times coming on.

KYD   But you'll be staying. Yes! They'll want to see if they can use you . . . again.

             (STONE *merely smiles at the implication. He pours a tankard of some warm liquid.*)

STONE   This is still hot. These spices! They must cost
                      a fortune.

KYD   Ingram will be up there now, sharpening his
                      red quill . . . he has these coloured quills from
                      strange tropical birds . . . He'll be writing to
                      the Queen's monkey . . . "Ralegh at Scadbury
                      expressly to renew his secret connection with
                      Marlowe and discuss with him atheistic
                      propositions, blasphemy and sedition." He'll
                      eke out a whole list of them and finish by
                      saying how outraged his master and mistress
                      were and how they asked Ralegh to cut short
                      his visit.

STONE   Why?

KYD   Why what?

STONE   Why should the Walsinghams use Ingram to
                      undermine Ralegh?

KYD   Why should *Audry* Walsingham . . .

STONE   All right. Why?

KYD   You can't see it?

STONE   No.

KYD   Herself. The Queen.

STONE   Yes?

KYD   Our Sovereign lady's childless and nearly
                      sixty. Who succeeds her is the only political
                      question worth discussing and that's
                      forbidden. (*Indicates the next room.*) Audry
                      Walsingham supports King James for the
                      throne. Ralegh doesn't.

STONE   Does Kit?

KYD   No. Despite the obvious. Keeps saying he'll
               go to Scotland but he won't. Can't stand
               James any more than Ralegh can. Little
               white-faced Caledonian runt shitting his
               padded, bullet-proof britches. "The sort of
               man who gives sodomy a bad name." This is
               Kit I'm quoting you understand.

STONE   Who does Ralegh support?

KYD   No one. Rumour says he wants a republic.
               Like Venice.

STONE   What was the School of Night?

KYD   I don't know. Nor should you.

STONE   I was trying to think why Ralegh allowed
               himself to be insulted. Whether Kit has some
               hold over him. They say the "school" was
               connected with some of the great names in the
               land.

KYD   Was it?

STONE   Northumberland.

KYD   The Wizard Earl? Quite likely.

STONE   I thought you might have been a member . . .

KYD   No. I wouldn't have been considered clever
               enough.

STONE   You say Kit was a spy?

               (KYD *sizes* STONE *up, then decides to be
               indiscreet.*)

KYD   Recruited by the Queen's Spymaster, no less
               . . . Tam's cousin, the late Sir Francis
               Walsingham.

STONE   When?

KYD   Back in '82.

                        (STONE *is surprised* MARLOWE *was recruited as
                        an undergraduate.*)

STONE   (*puzzled*) At . . . ?

KYD   (*nods*) Cambridge. They needed agents to spy
                        on English Catholic exiles in France . . .
                        listen in on their seditious plotting with Spain
                        to dethrone our sovereign Lady. Very
                        patriotic work . . .

                        (*He is feeling out* STONE'S *political attitude.*)

STONE   Ah yes.

KYD   They recruited Protestant divinity students on
                        the grounds that they'd know the form when it
                        came to posing as Catholics. And Kit . . .
                        don't laugh . . . was a divinity student. He
                        made several trips.

STONE   Is this known?

KYD   It is at Cambridge. The authorities tried to
                        refuse Kit his degree. Awarding a degree to
                        an atheistic divinity student with homosexual
                        tendencies was a bit strong . . . even for
                        Cambridge. But the reason they gave out was
                        Kit's mysterious absences when he should
                        have been studying. And you know what the
                        Walsinghams did? Had the Cambridge
                        authorities overruled by the Privy Council.

STONE   So Kit got his degree?

KYD   For a man who condemns power he seems to
                        get plenty on his side. And money . . .

STONE   For spying?

KYD   That . . . and patronage . . . bursaries . . .
                commissions . . . it all comes to Kit. I have
                been two years trying to get my present play
                written - but I only have theatre money to go
                on most of the time. And there's Henslowe,
                pays more for one damned costume hat than
                he does for a play. Oh yes . . . you can knock
                off two *Tamburlaines* and a *Faustus* before
                you're twenty five if you have Kit's friends.

STONE   Is he still . . . an agent?

KYD   Once they've got you they don't let you go.
                They've ruined him, in my opinion. There's a
                portrait of him at Corpus Christi College. He
                chose the inscription: "Quod me nutrit me
                destruit."

STONE   Er . . .

KYD   "Who feeds me, destroys me."

                (WALSINGHAM, AUDRY, ROSALINDA *and* FRIZER
                enter following a white-faced and enraged
                MARLOWE. *He speaks directly to* STONE,
                pointedly ignoring KYD.)

MARLOWE   We've been talking about you!

ROSALINDA   You see it suddenly came back to me where
                you and I met before . . .

                (*She gives* STONE *a hostile look.*)

KYD   (*to* MARLOWE) I'm going to London. I've
                crawled enough for money.

MARLOWE   (*still fixing* STONE *with his eye*) Catch up with
                Ralegh. There could be a few pieces of silver
                in it for you.

KYD   Well, two writers under one roof is one too
                many.

AUDRY	If you ask me it's two too many.
MARLOWE	Especially when there are three.
	(*The focus of attention moves to* STONE.)
ROSALINDA	*Tu lo sai, eh?* [You know it, eh?] You know . . . you know . . .
MARLOWE	Quiz. Which character, in which play, said: "My mouth shall be the parliament of England"?
	(STONE *smiles, half embarrassed, half irritated at this line of approach.*)
WALSINGHAM	Would you allow me to answer?
MARLOWE	Please Tam! I want it from him.
STONE	Jack Cade, the Kentish rebel.
MARLOWE	Which play?
KYD	*Harry the Sixth!* (*He is wondering what all this is about.*)
ROSALINDA	No! (*Points at* STONE.) He must answer!
STONE	*Harry the Sixth.*
MARLOWE	How can you be sure? Have you seen it . . . or acted in it?
STONE	I wrote it.
KYD	You!
ROSALINDA	Oh what's the point? He can see he's found out!
WALSINGHAM	I think Kit feels the need to construct a scene out of it.

MARLOWE   I only ask myself why the author of *Harry the Sixth* presents himself here as one Thomas Stone instead of . . . how d'you say it? Shag-Spur?

STONE   Shakespear.

KYD   Shakespear? You mean you wrote *Harry the Sixth*?

STONE   The better parts.

ROSALINDA   He knew I'd remembered! A house on the corner of Silver Street near London Wall . . . eh? I go to meet a friend . . . an Italian lady. I see you in the doorway . . . and I afterwards couldn't remember this strange English name . . . Shake-a-spear.

MARLOWE   Why tell us your name was Stone?

STONE   I didn't. Mr Frizer, when he hired me, read it in the playbill. It's my stage name. I shortened a name I once used as a pamphleteer . . . 'Touchstone' . . . 'the test of truth'.

ROSALINDA   Beautiful! *Meraviglioso!* [Wonderful!] Wonderful! You'd almost believe him!

STONE   My company had a problem. We thought it best to leave *Harry the Sixth* and William Shakespear in London. Some Kentish aldermen . . . we depend on them for our performing licences . . . they'd taken exception to my portrayal of Jack Cade as being too sympathetic. What stuck in their craw especially was that I'd allowed the swine-ish rebel son of a bricklayer to speak in blank verse!

               (MARLOWE *likes this. He begins to quote Henry the Sixth from memory.*)

MARLOWE   "And you that love the commons follow me . . . "

STONE   (*prompts*) "Now show yourselves men . . . "

MARLOWE   "Tis for liberty!
               We will not leave one lord, one gentleman;
               spare none but such as go in clouted shoon."

STONE   You've seen it?

MARLOWE   No . . . Ingram gets me pirate copies.

KYD   You'll be all right now. He thinks you're
               devious. He loves that. (*To* MARLOWE.) You'll
               want to study him won't you? Give him my
               room. Take it, sir. It has an appetising view
               of the kitchen gardens. Tam . . . you said I'd
               have a passport in case I'm stopped and
               searched.

               (FRIZER *hands a document to* KYD.)

WALSINGHAM   Also my note of hand for the expenses of the
               journey. I wish I could have done more, Tom.

KYD   Well . . . another takes my place. It seems
               you can no more rid yourself of playwrights
               than the City can rid itself of corpses.

ROSALINDA   Don't go into the City!

KYD   I don't mind the dead. I've some very good
               friends amongst them. Kit . . . I still have a
               box of your papers from the time I once gave
               you lodgings. What shall I do with them?

               (MARLOWE *ignores him.* KYD *waits then,
               furious, grabs his things and goes.*)

MARLOWE   Has he gone?

AUDRY   Gone, I think, is too small a word for it.
               Really Kit. If I were one of your fellow
               writers I, too, would use a false name.

STONE	Not 'false', Mistress Walsingham. 'Stage'. But I must admit I wouldn't have been eager to reveal myself on the strength of one play . . . not to the two who really started it all.
MARLOWE	Oh yes! You're "the Upstart Crow who dresses himself in our borrowed feathers."
STONE	And you're the "scoffing poet, born of Merlin's race".
MARLOWE	Are you a poet? You'll need to be now with the theatres closed.
STONE	I've been wanting to write a poem, yes.
WALSINGHAM	May I ask the theme?
STONE	The story of Venus and Adonis.
WALSINGHAM	What coincidence!
AUDRY	My, my, my!
MARLOWE	I'm writing Hero and Leander. Fate can't be denied, Tam. We're brought together to write two love poems in one house. (*To* STONE.) D'you need money?
STONE	Yes . . .
MARLOWE	Commission him!
ROSALINDA	No!
	(*There is something about* STONE *that troubles her.*)
	(*covering herself*) He may not want to.
MARLOWE	Oh I'm sure he does. Let's settle you in, Master Shake-Stone-Touch-Spear.

(STONE *flinches slightly as* MARLOWE *puts an arm round him to lead him away. They exit.*)

ROSALINDA   Whose man is he? Why is he here? You know! *Fa l'innocente!* [Pretending to be innocent.] Oh you know!

(ROSALINDA *gets no response. Exits.*)

AUDRY   Well? Whose man is he?

FRIZER   His own. I checked.

AUDRY   I say the Archbishop's.

FRIZER   I'd smell it.

WALSINGHAM   Perhaps you should put a listening tube in his room.

AUDRY   Then, at least, I might learn something about his names. D'you believe his story? About the Kentish magistrates?

FRIZER   No. But there's another explanation . . . one that he wouldn't want to advertise . . . assuming that he really is the writer Shake-spear.

WALSINGHAM   Why? Is there another Shake-spear?

FRIZER   I mean assuming it's not a double bluff.

AUDRY   Oh assume something, for pity's sake!

FRIZER   If he is the writer Shakespear, he might want to put a distance between himself and the family name because his father would be one John Shakespear, a glover who lives in a small town on the Warwickshire Avon. He's a suspected Catholic. And inclined to illness on Sundays.

AUDRY   Ah! A recusant!

FRIZER	His non-church attendance is quite conspicuous.
AUDRY	Is he on the list?
FRIZER	Yes. And I presume his son would do a lot to have his father cleared - or, at least, de-listed.
WALSINGHAM	I don't want him pressured. And I want no moves against Kit. This family will keep its hands clean in the matter.
FRIZER	The curious thing is that coincidence . . . of the two poems.
WALSINGHAM	Oh?
FRIZER	Kit working on Hero and Leander. In walks a man with Venus and Adonis.
WALSINGHAM	But then, it's not a question of 'In walks a man' is it? You chose him. Unless, unbeknown to you, he chose himself. Maybe he intended to come here all along . . . to be Merlin's apprentice.
AUDRY	We should be finding ways of making Merlin disappear, not allowing him an apprentice!
WALSINGHAM	I'll remind you, my love that Kit was one of my cousin's agents. He did dangerous work in France. Our royal mistress, herself, approved a document six years ago commending him for his service to the state. He's one of us. The service must never be seen to abandon an ex-agent. I simply want Kit to go abroad to safety. He fears that, if he did, his work would be suppressed. But if he had someone here he could trust, a play-wright, a poet, a partner . . . let them work together. Then we'll see.

(*He exits.* AUDRY *rounds on* FRIZER.)

AUDRY   My husband is still in Kit's bed. Yes! In his
               mind, he is! He knows what we have to do,
               but can't bring himself to do it. You'll have
               to take independent action. You're not family.
               So you can dirty your hands. Don't tell me
               about it. Do it. But always remember whose
               man you are.

               (*She pats his face sharply. The lights fade.*)

                            Scene Four

*Scadbury, three days later. A bed-chamber, simply
represented by a high, canopied bed with lamps burning
around it. A feeling, again, of Venice with the kind of African
ornaments that would have found their way through that city
to the west.*

It is past midnight. ROSALINDA *sleeps. In her hand the loose
sheets of paper bearing the first twenty or so verses of 'Venus
and Adonis'.*

MARLOWE *enters silently and stares at her, longing for
company through another wakeful night. He sees the papers,
stealthily removes them from her hand and begins to read,
full of curiosity and apprehension.*

Suddenly ROSALINDA *wakes, takes a scimitar from the
scabbard by the bed and puts the blade to* MARLOWE'S *throat.*

ROSALINDA   Give that back! It's not for you to read. It's
               not finished . . . he only wants you to read it
               when it's finished . . .

               (MARLOWE *doesn't move.* ROSALINDA *lowers the
               blade, helplessly.*)

MARLOWE   "Even as the sun with purple-colour'd face
               Had ta'en his last leave of the weeping morn,
               Rose-cheek'd Adonis hied him to the chase . . ."

(*He reflects a moment.* ROSALINDA *now fears that he will become jealous of* STONE'S *ability.*)

ROSALINDA   Let me have it. Please!

MARLOWE   Bring that lamp . . .

(*He now reads avidly as she, resignedly, brings the lamp nearer to him. He finishes reading.*)

Why does he show his work to you and not to me?

ROSALINDA   Because it's unfinished!

MARLOWE   When did he show it you?

ROSALINDA   Today.

MARLOWE   When? Tonight?

ROSALINDA   This morning.

MARLOWE   Impossible . . .

ROSALINDA   But he did . . .

MARLOWE   Have you actually seen him writing . . . been with him?

ROSALINDA   No.

MARLOWE   How could he have written so much in so short a time? Three days! All of them in our company. The first night he slept . . . or pretended to when I looked in. And last night . . . ?

(*He pauses and gives her a sardonic look.*)

ROSALINDA   Don't sneer at me!

MARLOWE	Last night he was discovering another Venus . . . in softer sheets than these . . . (*He touches her cheek with the poem.*)

ROSALINDA   *Che cosa vuoi dire?* [What are you saying?]

MARLOWE   Was it Ingram's idea you should take him to bed and pass on the pillow talk? Or is Touch using you?

(ROSALINDA *is hurt, vulnerable to his relentless harshness.*)

ROSALINDA   *Perchè mi tormenti cosí?* [Why torment me like that?] What am I to do? Mother of God, what am I to do? You have no use for me . . .

MARLOWE   But you don't even like him . . .

ROSALINDA   I always take men I don't like! You know that! (*Quietly.*) And you know why . . . What do I think it does? Help me to keep faith with you? I don't even feel he likes me. Or anybody. Or anything . . . except his work.

MARLOWE   If it is his work . . . It's not paper from this house.

ROSALINDA   Why should he bring someone else's work?

MARLOWE   It's what you'd have to do if you wanted to convince someone that you were the author of *Harry the Sixth* when you weren't the author of *Harry the Sixth*.

ROSALINDA   But we had to force him to admit it. He didn't try to convince us.

MARLOWE   But that's how to make it more . . . convincing. Either he has a mechanism in his brain that transfers his thoughts to paper, fair copied and corrected at will . . . or . . .

(*They hear a sound.*)

Are you expecting him?

(*Reluctantly she nods.*)

Touch!

(STONE *enters, smiling.*)

STONE   I heard you moving about . . .

MARLOWE   And you thought you were missing
                 something. (*To her.*) He's taking care of you
                 Leopardess . . .

STONE   I heard a horseman in the stableyard just now.

MARLOWE   Post. From Westminster. Comes at all hours.
                 This house never sleeps. I know all its night
                 sounds. (*Pause.*) I've read the verses . . .

STONE   I'm glad. I wanted you to. I'd appreciate your
                 help.

MARLOWE   The man who wrote this needs no help.

                 (STONE *avoids the implication.*)

STONE   What did you think?

MARLOWE   "And yet not cloy thy lips with loathed satiety,
                 But rather famish them amid their plenty,
                 Making them red and pale with fresh variety;
                 Ten kisses short as one, one long as twenty."

                 It has the essential prerequisite of a poem
                 seeking out a rich patron.

STONE   What prerequisite?

MARLOWE   Sex. In classical form, of course.

STONE   You don't think it's mine. And in a way it
                 isn't . . . once written. You could say it was
                 mine but isn't now . . . unless . . .

ROSALINDA   Unless?

STONE   Unless you're talking money - then it's mine.

                 (MARLOWE *likes this. He embraces* STONE.)

MARLOWE   At all events you're not a whingeing
                 constipated poet like poor Tom Kyd. Dear
                 Tom-arse! Bent double with the bitterness of
                 the world, shitting his little puppy pellets of
                 self pity and moral indignation. (*Gives him
                 the poem.*) I like it. Your Adonis is a pretty
                 boy.

                 (ROSALINDA *curls her arm round* STONE.)

ROSALINDA   But his Venus is a real woman!

MARLOWE   As I'm sure he's well aware. But what d'you
                 say, Africa? Can I trust him?

ROSALINDA   No . . . you trust only me!

MARLOWE   I meant as a fellow poet. To work with. D'you
                 write sonnets?

STONE   Yes.

MARLOWE   The Earl of Southampton's mother is looking
                 for a ream of sonnets addressed to her son -
                 possibly the prettiest boy in England. They
                 are to persuade him to marry and beget. Not
                 the subject I'd have chosen . . . there's more
                 than enough heterosexuality in the world . . .
                 but the money is in quite solemn quantities.
                 We'll write them together. At the same table.

                 (*An implication that* MARLOWE *still wants
                 assurance of* STONE's *identity.*)

ROSALINDA   I want my lover.

MARLOWE   Take him!

ROSALINDA   I mean I want him to myself.

MARLOWE   Perhaps we could share him.

ROSALINDA   Not this one. Anyway he won't.

MARLOWE   Can you be so sure? He might not but the
              other might.

ROSALINDA   Who?

MARLOWE   The one he carries on his back. Whenever
              Touch looks at you, have you noticed . . . you
              feel you're being watched from another
              quarter. He smiles, but the other doesn't. His
              familiar. His fetch. His other self. Now which
              is Tom and which is Will?

STONE   Piss!

MARLOWE   My dear Touch!

STONE   May your canine deity cock his leg against
              you! I am what I am, and only what I am.
              Please believe that . . .

              (ROSALINDA *hears something.*)

ROSALINDA   Voices . . .

MARLOWE   Maybe a letter from herself.

STONE   The Queen? Does she write to Walsingham?
              In person?

              (MARLOWE *eyes him shrewdly.*)

MARLOWE   Yes Touch. She does.

STONE   Has she been here?

MARLOWE   No. Scadbury's too small to support her and
                 her train. She only visits those she wants to
                 ruin. I saw her once, just once. I was in a
                 group, bowing low . . . Dog help me! And
                 suddenly I had an uninterrupted view of her
                 skirts. On the top layer . . . what d'you call
                 it? The over-mantle . . . there was a border of
                 little embroidered human eyes . . . a shoal of
                 them, rippling as she walked by. The eyes of
                 majesty that see all!

                 (*From somewhere in the house they hear a
                 commotion.*)

WALSINGHAM   (*off*) Kit! Kit! We have something . . . Kit, are
                 you there?

AUDRY   He's with *her*!

                 (ROSALINDA *quickly throws the scimitar to*
                 MARLOWE *who takes a stand by the door.
                 Enter* WALSINGHAM *and* AUDRY.)

WALSINGHAM   Don't be alarmed!

AUDRY   (*triumphant*) They've taken him!

STONE   Who?

WALSINGHAM   Ralegh. (*He reads a letter.*) From Ingram in
                 London: "On the instant of two in the
                 afternoon Sir Walter was taken from his house
                 and to the Tower. It is assumed the charge is
                 his covert marriage since his wife, Elizabeth
                 Throckmorton, is also taken. No charge of
                 atheism is heard of yet. I shall continue to
                 inquire."

AUDRY   So. He's there where he belongs! God save
                 our sovereign Lady! God save the Queen!

(*Her tone challenges* MARLOWE *to declare loyalty to the Queen. The others respond. He delays.*)

ALL   God save the Queen!

MARLOWE   Hmmm. Yes. Dog save the virgin bitch . . .

ROSALINDA   No, Kit! No!!

MARLOWE   The walking womb strikes back! Who'd have thought that same royal and ancient organ . . . unexplored, they tell us . . . untried, unvisited . . . that has been for so many years the Holy Grail of Europe is not so dried up yet that it can't take the head of an unfaithful favourite and squeeze it hard!

ROSALINDA   You give them what they want!

WALSINGHAM   All I want is Kit's safety. And I wish he'd make it easier for me! Soon they'll turn their attention to all who can help worsen the case against Ralegh. You're one. My old friend - I can only help you if you'll help yourself.

MARLOWE   Then make sure I'm not put to the torture. Otherwise I may not be able to help myself.

AUDRY   You give yourself away without torture!

WALSINGHAM   Whatever you say, Kit, my previous offers to you still stand. I will find you a place of safety. Only say the word. I beg you to consider the deadly seriousness of these people. You know the process: for every agent a counter-agent; for every counter-agent, ten informers; for every known informer, ten unknown. We can't keep track of them all. Once the net is fully spread I may not be able to help you.

(*Exit* WALSINGHAM *and* AUDRY.)

ROSALINDA   She'll make trouble.

MARLOWE   What with?

ROSALINDA   I'm afraid of her. And Ingram . . . he's her man, not Tam's.

MARLOWE   I'll match Ingram.

STONE   Was Tam a member of the School of Night?

(MARLOWE *eyes him with contempt.*)

MARLOWE   (*to* ROSALINDA) Get him away from here.

ROSALINDA   No. He's got to help me get you away.

STONE   She's right. You should go abroad.

MARLOWE   I thought you'd never say it! That's what you're here for, isn't it? To persuade me! To make Merlin disappear! That's what Tam's paid you for . . .

STONE   No.

MARLOWE   Only your keep?

STONE   I *agree* with him.

MARLOWE   Why??

STONE   Because I think you the greatest man in England. And because they burn atheists.

MARLOWE   They won't burn me. I'd make too great a stink.

STONE   They burned Francis Kett. He was your tutor at Corpus Christi, wasn't he?

(*For a moment this gives* MARLOWE *the feeling that* STONE *has been briefed on him. He lets it pass.*)

MARLOWE   Well . . . he was only a university man. There
               are quite a few surplus to requirements now.

               (*A cock crows. They all register the first light
               dawning. The beginnings of the dawn chorus.*)

ROSALINDA   *Constringilo a salvarsi!* [Make him go!] He
               must go! Make him go!

MARLOWE   Water . . .

STONE   What?

MARLOWE   Yes . . . Sir Water in his cell by the water . . .

ROSALINDA   Come home to my father's house!

MARLOWE   By the city of the water . . .

ROSALINDA   Venice! You've called it the city of cities.
               You've dreamed of going there.

MARLOWE   Have I?

ROSALINDA   You've told me! Many times!

               (MARLOWE *sniffs . . . his head back, turning
               slowly this way and that.*)

MARLOWE   I can smell water . . .   Shall I tell you why I
               can't leave Scadbury?

ROSALINDA   You have to leave! You have to!

MARLOWE   There's no question of my leaving. Going or
               not going . . . Venice or not Venice . . . It's in
               other hands than mine.

STONE   Whose?

MARLOWE   Let's see what you know about science. What
               is the transmutation of self?

STONE   A change of being . . .

MARLOWE   To what?

STONE   Another self . . .

MARLOWE   A higher self! A higher state! For how shall
             humanity benefit from science unless we are
             all transformed into something greater than
             we are? I have stumbled on certain presences
             . . . certain powers that will help me attain
             that state. They are centred on this house . . .
             now! The process is under way and must be
             completed!

ROSALINDA   If you don't believe in God, why do you
             believe in Satan?

MARLOWE   Not Satan. Science!

STONE   Kit . . . this increases the danger!

MARLOWE   What danger? This higher state, once
             attained, will make their most fearsome
             threats seem like the harmless gestures of
             distant children . . . (*To* ROSALINDA.) Take
             hands . . .

ROSALINDA   No!

MARLOWE   I need your strength . . . Don't be afraid.
             There's no evil.

             (*He takes* ROSALINDA'S *hand.* STONE *remains
             apart, watching intently.*)

             At this moment we occupy the space between
             dawn and morning. The spirits of the dead
             have returned to their graves and in these
             short, ever-lightening moments we, the living,
             who are set free to haunt the beginning of the
             day. This is the time of revelation. If you
             wake from sleep now you wake not in terror
             of night, but in awe of day. Not in the fear of

death but in the unbearable splendour of life
. . . of knowing you must live! You want to
cry out for seeing revealed your own
mortality, towering, worlds-high above you!
Or look down and find your feet on the verge
of the universe. You know that I and others
have made a secret study of the forbidden arts
. . . the knowledge that they . . . and *she* . . .
most want to suppress, fearing it might bring
to the common herd the powers of majesty.
We sons of cobblers, daughters of slaves! But
we have learned too much already and can't
be stopped! I have had signs . . . that what I
am to become will be purest gold compared to
the base metal I am now. I've seen the room.
I've seen a kind of bed where I could be lain
down as myself and raised as Homer . . . or
Virgil . . . or Dante! I've seen the agents of
that power . . .

(*During this the vision in the mind of the
room by the river has slowly appeared, three
figures standing.*)

 . . . still, silent, ready to reveal the future . . .
ready to make me the sign that I shall follow.

(*One of the figures raises his fist and beats
the air with a great booming sound again and
again as the lights fade to black. The sound
continues in the dark gradually becoming the
real sound of a real fist beating against a real
door.*)

Scene Five

Dogs barking. London. TOM KYD'S *room in some lodging
house. Minimally suggested . . . a door, a low trestle bed,
rickety table, masses of boxes of paper and loose papers
scattered about.*

It is dawn. Two city clocks chime four distantly. KYD *sits bolt upright in bed as lantern light streams through cracks in the door and someone hammers against it violently.*

He leaps from the bed pulling a blanket round his naked body. Looks around wildly, wondering what, if anything to hide.

SKERES   (*off*) Get it open! Queen's warrant! Refusal is treachery! One! Two! Three!

                   (SKERES *and* POLEY *charge the door and rush into the room. We are aware of a third shadowy figure outside the door.* SKERES *and* POLEY *are very tense, their first consideration is for their own safety, hidden dangers etc.* POLEY *takes a stance holding a pistol in both hands outstretched (modern regulation style) pointed at* KYD'S *head.* SKERES *has a heavy stick which he will use to beat against floor or furniture to unnerve* KYD. *They shout their commands and questions as a technique to disorientate him and get him to incriminate himself.*)

SKERES   Stand still! Show your hands!

POLEY   (*with pistol*) Show them! Don't move!

SKERES   Now, hands holding each corner!

POLEY   One hand to each corner!

                   (KYD, *puzzled at first, grasps each corner at the top of his blanket.*)

                   Slowly open the blanket . . . slow! Wider, wider!

                   (KYD, *back to the audience, opens out the blanket, so they can see he's naked and unarmed.* SKERES *lifts the back of the blanket with his stick.*)

Legs apart! Further!

SKERES	Where d'you keep 'em?
KYD	What? (*He tries to cover his genitals.*)
POLEY	Don't look at that! It's other weapons we want!
SKERES	Weapons! Quickly!
KYD	On the bed. Knife . . .
POLEY	Poinard! There . . .
KYD	I was going to tell you . . .
SKERES	Dagger, French origin, concealed in bedclothes . . .
KYD	No!
SKERES	Poinard, broken point, undeclared!
KYD	You don't wait. Who are you?

(*From downstairs a woman's voice.*)

WOMAN'S VOICE	(*off*) Tom! Are you all right? Tom!

(POLEY *moves to door, getting a slight nod from the muffled up man outside.* POLEY *calls down.*)

POLEY	Get it off the stairs, Mostyn!
MOSTYN'S VOICE	(*off*) Sir! Inside!
WOMAN'S VOICE	(*off*) Tom! Tom!

(*A door closes below. For the first time*
SKERES *lowers his voice.*)

SKERES   Officers of the Privy Council pursuant of the
           safety of our most sovereign Lady, the Queen
           and her realm of England. Do you resist this
           search?

KYD   What's it for?

POLEY   Close your blanket!

SKERES   Seditious libel. You've barred your door,
           refused entry, concealed weapons, withheld
           information and lewdly displayed your naked
           body to the affront of her majesty. Do you
           resist this search?

KYD   No.

           (POLEY *begins to search through papers.*)

SKERES   Your name is Kyd? Don't look at him! Kyd?

KYD   Yes . . .

SKERES   Poet?

KYD   Well . . . writer . . .

SKERES   Poet? D'you write verses?

KYD   Sometimes . . .

SKERES   On walls?

POLEY   (*quoting from a paper*) "The incestuous
           Queen hath taken poison."

KYD   It's a play. The queen in the play!

           (POLEY *goes on searching.*)

POLEY   You were seen at the Dutch churchyard
               yesterday.

KYD   No! I was here . . . except . . .

POLEY   You were identified shortly before certain
               seditious and libellous verses were painted on
               a nearby wall. You have already admitted that
               you write verses and there is paint on your
               right hand.

KYD   Ink! It's ink! I write with ink! Search! You'll
               find no sedition here. No libel. I have said
               nothing and say nothing against her Majesty!

SKERES   Or God? What are these?

KYD   Old papers. Scrap.

SKERES   But not thrown away! Turn and face the wall!

               (KYD *is forced to face away.* SKERES *hands a
               sheaf of papers to the shadowy third man who
               now enters and reveals himself as* INGRAM
               FRIZER. *He reads the papers by lantern light,
               then whispers to* SKERES.)

POLEY   Face the wall!

SKERES   Are these yours?

KYD   They were lent to me. Given . . . left . . .

SKERES   These are atheistic writings . . . are you an
               atheist?

KYD   No . . .

SKERES   D'you consort with atheists? D'you want a
               name? D'you consort with a man called
               Marlowe?

KYD   I know him . . .

SKERES   You shared a room two years ago. Are they
              his?

KYD   Oh no, I don't think so . . . (*Tries to make it
              sound light-hearted.*) He wouldn't leave *his*
              papers. They might be worth something one
              day . . .

POLEY   This is what will happen now. Listen
              carefully. You will be given a further
              opportunity to name him in a moment and
              your hesitation overlooked. If you don't
              you'll be taken to Bridewell prison and given
              a second opportunity to name him . . . but
              your first refusal goes against you. If you still
              refuse to name him you'll be taken below to
              be shown the instruments of torture . . . by
              iron, brass, chain, rope, leather, stone and
              water. And you'll have your last opportunity.

SKERES   Face the wall!

POLEY   You don't like the man. He has belittled you.
              Been hostile to you. You owe him nothing.
              Now. Are these papers his?

KYD   I don't think . . . Oh Kit! Kit! Kit!

              (KYD *tries to fight the convulsions that seize
              his body. Behind him,* FRIZER *takes paper and
              pen as the lights fade.*)

              Interval.

ACT TWO

Scene One

Scadbury. The formal garden at dusk. MARLOWE, STONE *and the* WALSINGHAMS *watch as a masked actor playing* HARLEQUIN *accompanies* COLUMBINE *on a lute as she sings an innocent Italian song of love.* COLUMBINE *is played by* ROSALINDA *who, in white make-up, is not immediately recognisable.*

Enter PANTALONE, *masked. He steals slowly upon* HARLEQUIN *in an almost sinister manner. Slowly they circle each other,* HARLEQUIN *still playing the lute.*

The effect is intended to disturb. Is this an innocent scene? Are the masked men a danger?

PANTALONE   *Oh, povera figliola! Togli le mani di dosso a questa figliola!* [Poor girl! Take your hands from this girl!]

                      (*He wheezes in the manner of the* PANTALONE *character.*)

COLUMBINE   *Signor Pantalone, 'io l'amo!* [But I love him!]

PANTALONE   *Impossibile!* [Impossible!]

                      (PANTALONE *now beats* HARLEQUIN, *then drags off* COLUMBINE. HARLEQUIN *changes the mood. He affects heart-broken sadness. Takes out a pistol. Puts it to his head. Pulls trigger. Nothing. He indicates that there must be rain in the air and the powder is damp. He gives the pistol to* AUDRY *to hold.* HARLEQUIN *takes out a rope and makes a noose which he slips over his head. He looks around in vain for something to tie the rope to. He tries to lift himself up on the rope, falling over in the attempt. He speaks to his onstage audience in Italian.*)

HARLEQUIN   *C'e' qualcuno fra lor signori che puó
               prestarmi aiuto?* [Would any member of the
               audience care to assist me?] *Lei forse, bella
               Signora?* [You maybe, beautiful lady?]

               (*He speaks to* AUDRY.)

MARLOWE   He asks for the assistance of a member of the
               audience.

HARLEQUIN   *Meglio ancora! Un volontario che si uccida
               cosi posso vedere come si fa!* [Even better, a
               volunteer to kill himself so I can see how it's
               done!]

MARLOWE   Will anyone volunteer to kill themselves and
               show him how it's done.

HARLEQUIN   *Vediamo, vediamo! Dove attacco la fune
               ostrega!* [Let's see! Let's see! There's
               nothing to attach the rope to!] *Nessuno che mi
               aiuta? Orbene mi uccidero di risate!* [Nobody
               to help? Well then, I'll die laughing!]

MARLOWE   On second thoughts, he's decided to die
               laughing . . .

               (HARLEQUIN *begins to tickle himself all over
               and laughs in the harsh, squawking manner of
               the character, stopping abruptly to grin, slyly
               and bow.* COLUMBINE *and* PANTALONE *join him
               for the final bow. The two male actors exit,
               thanking their audience.*)

ACTORS   *Vi ringrazio a nome di tutti di cosí grata
               audienza e vi saluto. Addio!* [On behalf of us
               all! Thank you for your help and I salute you.
               Adieu!]

ROSALINDA   Thank you! Thank you! Tristano and
               Bernadino give you all their gratitude for this
               applause. If only we had the whole company
               and I could play something serious as well. I

could do the Princess of Fez . . . without
makeup. I poison myself for love!

MARLOWE   Not the Princess of Fez.

ROSALINDA   Who is asking you?

WALSINGHAM   We are, Rosalinda. We'd love an encore.

ROSALINDA   Then we *shall* do an encore. I'll speak to
               them.

               (*She makes it clear she is doing it for*
               WALSINGHAM, *not* MARLOWE.)

MARLOWE   D'you see this Harlequin? How he caught us
               and landed us. That's what comedy is . . . the
               bait that hides the hook.

AUDRY   I thought it was something to laugh at.

MARLOWE   Laughter is merely the fish opening its mouth.

AUDRY   What d'you know of comedy?

MARLOWE   I know that we are never more vulnerable
               than when we laugh. So as things are I'll try
               to keep a straight face.

WALSINGHAM   But what is the hook?

MARLOWE   The purpose.

WALSINGHAM   What purpose?

MARLOWE   Of comedy . . . or any play. To expose the
               world's evil and madness. Of course, I could
               be wrong. For instance, William Shakespear
               thinks me wrong . . . and if William
               Shakespear thinks I'm wrong then in all
               humility, it is just possible that I could be
               wrong!

STONE	I thought we'd agreed that, since the plague continues to keep the theatres closed,we'd leave William Shakespear aside for a while.
MARLOWE	Oh . . . take him out, dust him off and let him give an opinion.
STONE	I think what you call the purpose of a play is simply your purpose. And that if there is something separate from the play, called the writer's purpose . . . then this could damage the play.
AUDRY	Well, well . . .

(MARLOWE *is angered by the careful way* STONE *replies.*)

MARLOWE	He means . . . the good William means . . . that, while comedy should conceal a hook, we should all be allowed to wriggle off it.
STONE	But what if you only want to feed the fish . . . not catch them?

(MARLOWE *is disturbed by this . . . then recovers.*)

MARLOWE	We shouldn't discuss plays. We should dedicate ourselves to poetry. Let the theatres stay closed! And we'll remain here . . . under this moon . . . these country nights. Our Arcadia. Our Academy. Our star-lit study where we forget those who work against us . . . or seek to ensnare us . . . (*Indicating* ROSALINDA.) Even with the sweetest of earthly delights. To hell with plays!

(ROSALINDA *feels herself rejected.*)

ROSALINDA	To hell with you! Write your poetry . . . with him. Your *Venus and Leander - Hero and Adonis*! Who needs you? I don't need you! In the Commedia we don't have writers. We take

a story and *we* make the words. The actors! We improvise. We do it! We're free of you!

(ROSALINDA *exits.* AUDRY *turns the thought on to* MARLOWE.)

AUDRY Free of *you*? How could she be so heartless?

STONE But can they ever be free?

AUDRY Who?

STONE The actors . . . free of the writer. For if the actors devise the play where is the unique vision of the mind that every play must have? Unique is one. I. Me. Singular. Not the many.

MARLOWE Surely he can't mean the author's purpose.

STONE Not my purpose . . . My mind's purpose.

WALSINGHAM You must explain the difference . . .

STONE One is that which I create. The other is created for me. One I know. The other . . . never.

(WALSINGHAM *is aware of* MARLOWE *momentarily unnerved by this.*)

WALSINGHAM But couldn't two people share the same vision . . . as we say two minds with but a single thought?

STONE (*aware of his concern*) Two perhaps . . . but three? Six? Ten?

MARLOWE The Pope would say a million can share one vision.

STONE Yes.

AUDRY Oh come! You're not agreeing with the Bishop of Rome?

STONE   That a million could share a vision, yes. But
               not create it.

AUDRY   So when a congregation kneels in prayer
               nothing is created?

               (WALSINGHAM *loses patience with his wife's
               inquisitorial manner.*)

WALSINGHAM   He is talking about theatre . . . not theology!
               The million is the audience which shares the
               vision it cannot itself create. I am honoured
               that two such men should discuss such matters
               at my house, in my domain. We must ask
               ourselves, who give service in the defence of
               the realm, why do we do it? Not for personal
               gain . . . or for its own sake . . . but so that in
               this country under Her Majesty, philosophy
               and the civilised arts can be pursued free of
               dogma . . .

               (*He sees something across the lawn.*)

               Horsemen!

FRIZER   Where?

WALSINGHAM   The lodge wall. Those shadows by the fig
               tree.

STONE   Three of them . . .

WALSINGHAM   Someone crossing the lawn . . .

STONE   Rosalinda . . .

MARLOWE   So. Our encore.

               (*Enter* ROSALINDA *swiftly but quietly, trying to
               appear untroubled.*)

ROSALINDA   Kit! They have a warrant.

MARLOWE   What - are they closing the show?

WALSINGHAM	Who are they?
ROSALINDA	Hers! One has the coat of arms . . .
FRIZER	It'll be Maunder. Queen's Messenger.
ROSALINDA	(*to* MARLOWE) You're to go before her council in the morning.
WALSINGHAM	I'll speak to them.
ROSALINDA	I said I didn't think he was here! You could slip away while he's talking to them. Tristano and Bernadino go to Dover tomorrow. He can be one of them! He speaks Italian!
AUDRY	(*in quick contempt*) He has no passport.
ROSALINDA	I kept my father's! I still have it. You could take his name!
MARLOWE	I've looked to accomplish many things but not to be a father. Tam . . . wait for me. Well . . . all arcadias end like this, with a messenger. (*To* STONE.) After Apollo, Mercury. (*To* WALSINGHAM.) I won't come between you and your knighthood. But see that they treat me as a gentleman.
	(MARLOWE *exits with* WALSINGHAM, ROSALINDA *and* STONE. AUDRY *and* FRIZER *contain their relief . . . speaking covertly.*)
AUDRY	It's done!
FRIZER	I thought they'd never get here . . .
AUDRY	I could sing!
	(AUDRY *suddenly, violently kisses* FRIZER. *The lights fade.*)

Scene Two

Westminster. Prison Bars. MARLOWE *at a table. Candlelight.*

Distant sounds of dogs barking and howling. MARLOWE *looks up. Listens to the sound.*

MARLOWE   A little room. Close to the river. So close the waters enter through the stones. Corpse liquor!

                      (*He sprinkles a cloth with some antidote to plague and presses the cloth to his mouth and nose. He looks up.*)

                      You hear that? The dogs of London mourning for their dead. Crying for masters and mistresses in whose slime that other deity has planted roses. They sneeze, fall down, burst from the houses and lie stacked like dolls in the street. He looks down, feet astride, his black tent flapping as the wind blows in Heaven's fields. What have they done? These base-born common people . . . what cataclysmic evil? What malignant thing to deserve this massacre? Is it that in the innermost secrecy of their hearts they too were atheists? Well Dog? You're not a faithful dog. You wouldn't bring me here if you were. You're a cunning dog. A cheeky dog! I show you my vision of self-transformation and pray to you and you bring me to Westminster! What transformation into something better could anyone expect of Westminster?

                      They work the other way round here. Here, the gold of human aspiration is rendered into lead. So what will they do to me? Keep me in prison. At least I'd die whole. I wouldn't be burned. In Venice they drown you. Well, they would, wouldn't they? Better than burning! Even hung, drawn and quartered you're still recognisably human . . . but burned . . . it takes away all connection. There's nothing left but a grinning parody, some twisted stump of charcoal, to tell what you once were. That's why they prescribe it for the crime of thought. So nothing remains. Oh Almighty Dog, who fears the flames more than we do, save us from burning. If I knew for certain that I was convicted of atheism then I'd quickly confess some crime of treason. You only get the knife and rope for that! When was it . . . yesterday that Rosalinda said she'd once acted the Princess of Fez? In that play the Princess's lover has his heart cut out and shown him just before he dies. They say the hangman at Tyburn can do it . . . cut your heart out so fast it's still pumping in his hand! Better than burning! In the last, bright instant of life to see your own heart in front of you . . . out of your body, free as a bird! Beating in the sun!

(*A key is turned in a lock.*)

RALEGH'S VOICE (*off*) Stay by that door. I'll take the keys.

WARDER'S VOICE (*off*) Sir!

(*Enter* RALEGH.)

MARLOWE Walter! I was expecting *them*.

RALEGH Dear boy, I am *them*. Well that's how you classified me last time we met. Is this a place for mighty Tamburlaine?

MARLOWE I'm not a prisoner . . . just waiting to be seen.

(RALEGH *notes this hint of self-delusion.*)

Has she let you go?

RALEGH I bought my release. I tried pleading, petitions . . . even poetry . . . but in the end it had to be money - that's something she really takes seriously. Especially eighty thousand pounds.

MARLOWE   You could buy every prisoner in England for
               that!

RALEGH   My Portuguese prize money from the Madre
               de Dios, taken by my sweet Roebuck. I gave
               the Queen my share as well as hers . . . and
               more . . . but she still won't see me. I'm
               paroled . . . as you are. You do realise you're
               free to go?

MARLOWE   How?

RALEGH   Tom Walsingham's bailed you out.

MARLOWE   But I haven't seen them yet!

RALEGH   They won't see you. Not today. Tom's
               arranged it so that you only have to report
               each morning until told otherwise.

MARLOWE   I must see them!

RALEGH   (*keenly interested*) Why?

MARLOWE   To know what they've got!

RALEGH   They've got what you left in Tom Kyd's
               room. Don't you remember what it was?

               (MARLOWE *senses* RALEGH *is fishing for
               information.*)

MARLOWE   Yes. Some mildly "blasphemous" writings I
               copied once. Harmless stuff! It wasn't even
               atheism. What sort of people are they paying
               these days? They can't convict on that!

RALEGH   If that's the case, why so agitated?

MARLOWE   Because they could have planted something!
               And dear Tom-arse would have said it was
               mine.

RALEGH   I was about to set off for Dorset when I heard
              you were taken. I've ridden hard to get here.
              In my present situation I risk a great deal by
              seeing you. We're both in danger and we can
              help one another. You're right about what
              they have upstairs . . . nothing. But it's
              enough to hold you till they have something
              better. What else could there have been in
              Tom Kyd's room that they missed?

MARLOWE   Ask Tom-arse! He'll tell you anything.

RALEGH   They *are* asking him. Now. He's under torture
              at Bridewell.

MARLOWE   I thought he named me to escape torture!

RALEGH   You've forgotten how things are done. They
              promise they won't torture you if you tell all
              you know and when you do they torture you
              just the same in case you might know
              something else.

MARLOWE   What has he said?

RALEGH   Nothing by yesterday evening . . . but the
              night was long . . . They'll search his room
              again and take it to pieces this time. I could
              have my man round there, ahead of them if
              you tell me where he should look.

MARLOWE   There's nothing else.

RALEGH   You know what I mean! I mean that list of
              names and places . . . those minutes . . . that
              log . . . whatever you want to call it . . . that
              record of the proceedings of the School of
              Night.

MARLOWE   The school that you say never existed?

RALEGH   If they're not at Kyd's where are they?
              They're not at Scadbury, I know that.

MARLOWE   Why? Did you send someone to search?

               (*Silence.*)

               We all swore not to keep records. How can
               there be any?

RALEGH   You remember Chomley . . . Richard
               Chomley . . . one of your "converts"?

MARLOWE   *Our* converts . . .

RALEGH   He's confessed. He's talked. They have him
               now! Telling them he attended atheistic
               lectures of yours and that, amongst unnamed
               "others" in the audience was myself! He also
               says records were kept by you. What was said.
               Where it was said and by whom. Names!
               That's what they want. Names. My name.

MARLOWE   So you think I broke faith? That I took
               names?

RALEGH   Oh Kit! In your position I'd have done it for
               the money! For those documents I'd pay a
               thousand guineas. Northumberland would
               double it. And one or two others . . . who
               wouldn't like the world to know the opinions
               they once held in their gilded Cambridge
               youth.

MARLOWE   Well. I've no such records.

RALEGH   Then I pity you. If you had we could destroy
               them. If you haven't they'll do it the other
               way. Pick the names out of you one by one.

MARLOWE   They could do that in any case.

RALEGH   My Angelica still has to keep me at arm's
               length . . . though it hurts and wounds her to
               do so! She fears these accusations may be
               proved. But if I could convince her that no
               evidence existed . . . that the School of Night

was never real . . . only a thing of the mind,
she'd take me back and you'd be safe.

MARLOWE   The things of the mind are the only things
that are real! You were one of us once. You
know that the fight for scientific
understanding and knowledge is the fight
against God and the fight against God is the
fight against her!

RALEGH   Get me those papers!

MARLOWE   Yes. You can have them . . . if you'll include
me in your grand design. Religion and
philosophy wasn't all we discussed in the
School of Night, was it?

RALEGH   What grand design?

MARLOWE   To set up a republic on the Venetian model -
led by the most powerful families in the land.
Including yours!

RALEGH   If all the world and love were young,
And truth in every shepherd's tongue . . .

MARLOWE   If I thought that there was the smallest chance
that England could be reborn in understanding
and inquiry, a republic of poetry and power,
co-existing - I'd live and die for it!

RALEGH   Would you, Kit, would you? Those papers.
Those names . . .

MARLOWE   There are no names!

RALEGH   Of course there are names! Those papers must
contain 'names'. If they didn't, what would
you be bargaining with?

MARLOWE   Our love.

          (A knock at the outer door, off stage.)

RALEGH   (*calls*) Yes! Presently! (*To* MARLOWE.) They'll
                ask you to sign a release paper in a moment,
                telling you to report here every morning and
                forbidding you to travel more than three miles
                from the court. You can't return to Scadbury.
                I don't see you taking up your old quarters at
                Tom Kyd's. Find a good hiding place, because
                if I discover that those papers contain names
                I'll find where you are and have you killed
                within the hour!

                (*He exits.*)

MARLOWE   Now Dog . . . stay by me. Come to heel.
                We'll cross the river. We'll go to the theatre.
                To the Rose. It's closed, but I think it may
                open for me.

                (*The lights fade.*)

                        Scene Three

*Behind the stage of the Rose Theatre which has been shut and
barred for some months by order during the plague.*

*A vast jumble of props forms the background. A cart, a
cannon, a throne, a mouth of hell big enough for the damned
to walk through, shields, spears, drums, etc, all gathering
dust on this warm, still sunlit day.*

*We should be conscious of the open sky beyond the backstage
area, with strong shafts of sunlight illuminating the scene.*

Insects drone. ROSALINDA *sprinkles liquid from a bowl around
the floor then scatters herbs against the plague. She is
watched by* STONE, *stretched out in the sun, a manuscript in
his hand. He recites Shakespeare's sonnet No. 132.*

STONE   "Thine eyes I love, and they, as pitying me,
                Knowing thy heart torments me with disdain,
                Have put on black and loving mourners be,
                Looking with pretty ruth upon my pain.
                And truly not the morning sun of heaven

Better becomes the grey cheeks of the east,
Nor that full star that ushers in the even,
Doth half that glory to the sober west,
As those two mourning eyes become thy face . . .

(MARLOWE *has entered, unseen by them, with
two swords. He listens to the sonnet with an
inner sense of defeat. When it's over, he
changes the mood, throwing one sword to*
STONE.)

O! let it, then, as well beseem thy heart
To mourn for me, since mourning doth thee
                                        grace,
And suit thy pity like in every part.
Then will I swear beauty herself is black,
And all they foul that thy complexion lack."

(ROSALINDA *stands stock-still, gazing at him
but her look betrays her anguish that she
can't love him.*)

MARLOWE   Here. Have you ever used one?

STONE   Only for exercise. And in plays, of course.

MARLOWE   Oh Rose! Sweet Rose. Where are your armies
               now? Look, I'm talking about going armed.
               You don't even carry a dagger.

STONE   No . . .

MARLOWE   If you consider yourself a gentleman - and
               you should - it's necessary to be armed. It's
               expected of you. And it's worth being thought
               a gentleman. Your word counts for more in a
               court of law. Anyway every actor should go
               armed. You never know who might take
               against a performance.

               (*They take guard.*)

               You're a gentleman. What are you?

STONE   A gentleman.

ROSALINDA   Stop playing games!

MARLOWE   It's no game. You know I once spent time in
             prison for fighting in the streets.

STONE   I had heard . . .

MARLOWE   I came between a man and his attacker. It's
             what you're doing now.

ROSALINDA   I shall go to Ralegh. I'll tell him if you won't.
             Why do you care who has these papers? I
             know where to look!

STONE   Does she?

MARLOWE   (to ROSALINDA) Now we shall know if he's
             Walter Ralegh's man . . . within the hour.

STONE   Couldn't you copy them?

MARLOWE   What?

STONE   These papers . . .

MARLOWE   What papers? She only thinks she knows.

STONE   Why keep up this pretence when your life's at
             stake?

MARLOWE   Because my life's at stake! As long as there's
             no evidence they can't move.

             (*They fence.* ROSALINDA *sits trembling, seeing
             no way out. Suddenly she cries out.*)

ROSALINDA   You have no right to say that! No right! I
             would never give you away to him! What am
             I? What am I? *Condannata* - Condemned? Is
             that what I am? Am I condemned to follow
             you?

MARLOWE   The machiavel has no Magdalene. You must
                 set yourself free.

ROSALINDA   Nothing can set me free. My mother was a
                 slave! A south wind blew last night. I thought
                 of her. Chained! Bought by my father in the
                 market place. For money! Venetian money!
                 Why didn't he fight? Not pay for her like
                 meat but take his sword and cut those chains!
                 And if they'd both died for it on the spot and
                 I'd never been on the earth that would have
                 been better. Better than this!

                 (STONE *hears a sound.*)

MARLOWE   Here! It's cocked. Be careful!

                 (*He hands* STONE *a pistol.*)

STONE   Ingram?

                 (*As they ease forward they hear the rattle of a
                 pebble hitting the outer wall. Another pebble
                 thrown. They move slightly towards the sound.
                 Then from the other side, behind them,
                 unseen, enter* POLEY *and* SKERES. *We recognise
                 them as the two officers who searched* KYD'S
                 *room. We see one of them toss a pebble over
                 the heads of the trio.* ROSALINDA *senses their
                 presence and turns.*)

ROSALINDA   *Chi è là?* [Who's there?]

                 (*As* STONE *turns to fire,* SKERES *leaps forward
                 to grab or knock his arm so that the shot goes
                 in the air.* STONE *struggles with him and they
                 begin to fence.* MARLOWE *and* ROSALINDA
                 recognise the two men and stand and watch.
                 STONE *puts up a spirited but ungainly
                 display.*)

SKERES   Hey! Hey! Hey! No sir! No sir, no! Friend . . .
                 friend . . .

ROSALINDA   Stop them! Fools!

POLEY   (*giving commentary*) Graze disengage . . .
                 circular parry . . . don't know what to call
                 that one . . .   `

                 (*By now* STONE *has realised that the men are
                 not enemies; the sword droops in his hand.*
                 SKERES *deftly disarms him, the sword falling
                 to the ground.* POLEY *applauds.*)

POLEY   Well played sir! What? Eh, Christopher?
                 Style! Body swerve! Eye on the blade!

MARLOWE   You realise this place is supposed to be
                 empty?

POLEY   (*points the way he came with* SKERES) You left
                 your backside open boy. Never do that.

ROSALINDA   Someone could be killed like this!

POLEY   Scuzi! Scuzi! Smile, majesty. Smile. I dream
                 of your smile, d'you know that?

                 (MARLOWE *introduces them to* STONE.)

MARLOWE   Nick Skeres. Robyn Poley. Two of
                 Walsingham's villains and cony catchers. I
                 say Walsingham's . . . "Anybody's" would be
                 nearer the truth . . .

ROSALINDA   What if someone heard the shot?

SKERES   Round here? They'd think it was some poor
                 sod taking the quick way out . . .

POLEY   There's not a house unboarded for two streets.
                 Good place to lie low, the old flower!
                 (*Referring to the theatre by its nickname.*)
                 I've had some laughs here!

ROSALINDA   What d'you want?

POLEY   Sweet bud! To look after you. We need a
tighter grip on things, as the boy female part
player said to the Jesuit priest. Jesting, sirs . . .
only jesting. As a matter of fact we're the
advance guard.

MARLOWE   Oh?

SKERES   He's a goer, your sonneteering friend here. I
nearly got the three quatrains and the final
couplet just now.

ROSALINDA   I wish you had!

SKERES   Bit too close to the old joke for my liking:
"never-touched-me-now-nod-your-head".

(SKERES *mimes his head falling off.*)

POLEY   Fights like a Switzer. You know "I'm-a-
professional-bugger-your-poncey-footwork!"
(*To* ROSALINDA.) Scuzi!

SKERES   No. Not a Switzer . . . (*To* MARLOWE.) Holds
himself like you. Bit after the North French
style. Rheims, was it?

(MARLOWE *makes a move towards him.*)

Hey! Keep him away. None of that! Hold on
to your shirt flaps!

(STONE *has picked up his sword and suddenly
laughs.*)

Whassermatter? Come on . . . Listen to him.
Did I say something?

STONE   It's buttoned! The sword!

(*Shows him the sword tip.*)

It's a property . . . a stage prop!

SKERES   Well, if I'd have known I'd have done the
              death of Pyramus!

POLEY   No seriously . . . seriously . . . you'll find it
              works better with a point on it.

SKERES   As the female woodpecker said to the male . . .

POLEY   Ralegh's men . . . they not only have points
              they have 'em venomed . . . "pointed with
              poison", you might say. Did you know that?

              (STONE *has suddenly quietened. He shakes his*
              head . . . having recognised something in
              what POLEY *said.*)

              Well with the venom you don't even have to
              start a fight. Snick in the leg . . . you hardly
              know it's happened . . .

ROSALINDA   Don't talk about it!

POLEY   (*listening*) Wait! (*Pause.*) It's them. So. Here
              we are to take you away . . .

MARLOWE   What?

POLEY   (*to* SKERES) You do the honours.

              (*He exits to let the others in.* SKERES *looks*
              uncomfortable, expecting KIT'S *anger.*)

MARLOWE   Nick! Take me where?

SKERES   Deptford. Tomorrow. You take ship to
              Holland. Pick up a Venetian trader at the
              Hook . . .

ROSALINDA   (*delighted*) We go to Venice?

SKERES   Well . . . it's your place he's to lie low in,
              isn't it? Your father's passport he'll have. Got
              it with you?

ROSALINDA	Yes! Yes! Oh yes!
	(*Enter* WALSINGHAM, AUDRY, FRIZER *with* POLEY.)
MARLOWE	You as well mistress! Has everybody been disposing of me?
WALSINGHAM	We have to act very urgently now Kit. There's a report on you . . .
MARLOWE	Who ordered it?
FRIZER	Queen's monkey . . .
	(MARLOWE *turns his back and walks away*.)
AUDRY	Oh leave him! Let him stew! (*To* MARLOWE.) Ingram has intercepted a report that now will not reach their Lordships till tomorrow and by doing so he's probably saved your life . . . which, as far as I'm concerned, is exceeding his duty! You mouth!
WALSINGHAM	He did so at my direction. Could we please look calmly at what has to be done? Let him see it . . .
	(FRIZER *offers the report*. MARLOWE *refuses*.)
MARLOWE	Who wrote it?
FRIZER	Richard Baines.
MARLOWE	Baines! Oh come on!
WALSINGHAM	Kit . . .
MARLOWE	Remember Flanders? That man'd have been on the slab if I hadn't stepped in!
SKERES	No honour among spies boy.

WALSINGHAM	On the contrary, that is precisely what there must be. Read some of it . . .
AUDRY	I wouldn't!
FRIZER	"Containing the opinions of Christopher Marlowe concerning his damnable judgement of religion and scorn of God's word. He affirms that Moses was but a juggler and that one Harriot, Sir Walter Ralegh's man, can do more than he."
MARLOWE	Has Ralegh seen it?
WALSINGHAM	Yes . . .
FRIZER	"That Christ deserved to die better than Barrabas and that the Jews made a good choice . . . that the first beginning of religion was only to keep men in awe . . . that the disciples John and Jesus were bedfellows and committed the act of sodomy . . . that all they who love not tobacco and boys are fools . . ."
AUDRY	Let them take him!
WALSINGHAM	Kit. It names as witness Richard Chomley, who will give evidence concerning the School of Night. It doesn't cite the School but he will. It ends: "I think all men in Christianity ought to endeavour that the mouth of so dangerous a member may be stopped." All that concerns us now is that this . . .

(Takes the report from FRIZER *and puts it in* MARLOWE'S *hand.)*

	. . . will bring you to questioning and, I would think most certainly, to trial. But, of course, as you know perfectly well, there are those who will not let you come to trial for fear of your incriminating them . . .
MARLOWE	Ralegh's named in it already . . .

FRIZER   He's paid me to see his name is taken out.

WALSINGHAM   He's a frightened man. That's why I've asked
                Nick and Robyn to be with you now at all
                times. Be in court in the morning as though
                nothing was unusual. Ingram can hold up the
                report for twenty four hours. Then they'll ride
                with you to Deptford and you'll be on the
                afternoon tide.

ROSALINDA   With me?

WALSINGHAM   Not in the same ship . . .

MARLOWE   If she stays she'll be taken . . .

STONE   I'll hide her. Trust me.

                (ROSALINDA *nods to* MARLOWE.)

ROSALINDA   I'm too much known with you. Too easily
                remembered. I'll give you away!

MARLOWE   How can I cut and run and leave others at
                their mercy? And you Tam. Are you to
                commit treason for me?

WALSINGHAM   No, my good friend. Not the way we've
                planned it.

                (*He nods to* POLEY, *who looks doubtfully at*
                STONE.)

POLEY   D'you want him to hear?

WALSINGHAM   Yes. He must.

POLEY   It's called Merlin's final appearance. Or the
                cobbler's farewell. You're going to die in
                Deptford. Dead man's switch. That's what
                we've been doing for two days . . . looking
                for a corpse that'll pass for you.

MARLOWE   You have one?

SKERES   It's hard to find anything that hasn't died of
               plague, these days. Ingram got him in the end.

FRIZER   He's off a Baltic merchantman. A Polack.
               Died yesterday.

MARLOWE   So. What kind of death do I die?

SKERES   You drown. We'll dump the Polack's body in
               the river, pull him out as soon as you've
               sailed and say he's you. We got some of your
               clothes from Scadbury to dress him in. Don't
               worry . . . not the velvet.

POLEY   We'll identify the corpse as yours . . . no one
               knows you in Deptford do they?

MARLOWE   Yes.

POLEY   Then we'll keep it between ourselves. Come
               on Kit! We've done it before and those who
               "died" are still alive and well. You'll be in
               your safe house and he'll be down under in St
               Nicholas' churchyard.

SKERES   They're used to drownings at Deptford.

FRIZER   In any case, we're able to set up the coroner.

MARLOWE   How?

FRIZER   You'll have died "within the verge" that is,
               within twelve miles of the royal presence. So
               it has to be handled by Danby, the Queen's
               coroner.

WALSINGHAM   I've spoken with him.

MARLOWE   He's not going to go against her?

WALSINGHAM	When will you accept that only the Archbishop requires your trial and execution? Not the Queen. Danby has instructions.
MARLOWE	Whose instructions?
WALSINGHAM	She'll know nothing.

(MARLOWE *moves away, thinking.*)

MARLOWE	If I'm dead what happens to my work?
WALSINGHAM	It's less likely to be suppressed . . .
MARLOWE	My future work! Or don't I have a future?
WALSINGHAM	(*to* STONE) Tell him what we discussed.
MARLOWE	Ah! Well, well!
STONE	I knew nothing of this switch. We discussed in general terms some days ago that I should offer myself as your go-between.
MARLOWE	D'you mean . . . my agent? My dear Touch!
ROSALINDA	We'll have a code . . . when I write to him.
MARLOWE	How exciting!
STONE	She can tell me when you have some work finished. I'll come to Venice. Get your instructions and bring the manuscript home.
MARLOWE	I've got the very code name! "Wormale". Anagram of Marlowe. A critic called it me once. Wormale! And if you anagram "Christopher" you get "Hithercorps". I shall be Wormale Hithercorps.
AUDRY	Wonderful! That should keep us guessing. No sooner has Christopher Marlowe departed this life than the Rose Theatre is suddenly deluged with play after play by Wormale Hithercorps.

MARLOWE   *(wistfully)* Play after play! Can Venice work
               miracles?

ROSALINDA   Yes!

STONE   It's been suggested I have your plays
               produced alongside mine . . .

MARLOWE   Wait a minute! D'you mean under your name?

STONE   Yes.

MARLOWE   Which name?

               (STONE *smiles.*)

STONE   My own.

MARLOWE   But how will you explain the difference? Who
               is going to accept that your 'vision' and mine
               could proceed from the same mind?

WALSINGHAM   Surely, there are similarities . . .

MARLOWE   No! He holds his mirror to humanity. I look
               behind the mirror.

AUDRY   What? Are we to stand here discussing
               dramatic criticism? As far as I'm concerned
               the world would be well rid of its geniuses!
               To hell with poets! (*To* MARLOWE.) Well,
               mouth? If you're going to reject our offers
               say so.

MARLOWE   Nick, Robyn. Tomorrow we go to Deptford.

               (*He makes as if to exit.*)

AUDRY   One moment! This isn't finished. There's
               something we must have in return.

MARLOWE   I thought there might be . . .

FRIZER   The names. The list.

MARLOWE   There are no names! No list! All I did after
          each meeting was write down from memory
          every opinion, statement, dispute, idea that I
          could hold in my mind. For the first time in
          my life I'd walked into a place where people
          were discussing the truth! The truth as
          forbidden by God, like knowledge in the
          Garden of Eden. And it tasted so sweet! Not
          the posturing and logic chopping of the
          university . . . not the craven self-censorship
          that passes for truth in public life! You stood
          naked to each other, each able to betray his
          fellow. But no one did! And that, too, was
          truth. So I kept no names. None. Just what
          was said. But I'm not going to let them have
          it. They'd destroy it all, names or not. They
          fear the idea more than they fear the thinker!
          I want to take those thoughts and turn them
          into something you (*To* STONE.) could never
          put your name to! When civilisation looks
          back and sees the crevasse we made across
          Europe and the world . . . this crack that runs
          through the remotest town and village. (*To*
          STONE.) You know it! Two Gods. Two credos.
          Two sets of lies. The purists and the zealots
          coming into their own on both sides.
          Oppressors clothed in the robes of divine
          authority. The state herding its people by law
          into the churches and forcing them to kneel
          before an altar that conceals the rack. I want
          them to know that there were some who spoke
          . . . and some who continue to believe that the
          only sin is ignorance.

          (*The light has already faded through the
          scene to twilight.*)

Scene Four

The same, just before dawn. STONE *sits in foreground,
writing. He is making a copy of Hero and Leander by lantern
light.*

In the background ROSALINDA *is asleep on a gilded classical couch, covered in gorgeous robes from the costume store.*

In the background SKERES, *blanket round him, drinks wine sleepily.* MARLOWE *enters, pale, drunk and with blood on his hands.*

MARLOWE   Blood! There's a bottle of it in there.

                (*He holds up a bottle.*)

                Give me the days when I could watch them
                walk this stage, act, bleed, die, go off for a
                steak supper and argue the toss about the
                day's rehearsal.

                (SKERES *crosses to him.*)

SKERES   Where d'you piss?

MARLOWE   (*indicates off stage*) There's a row of helmets
                from Pompey the Great.

SKERES   You made a mistake, telling them there are no
                names.

MARLOWE   What 'sit marrer?

SKERES   I'd have kept them by me, just in case. I knew
                an agent who worked for one of her majesty's
                ministers who swore he owed his life to the
                claim that he knew the whereabouts of a shirt-
                sleeve stained with the blood of Mary Queen
                of Scots . . . from her execution, I mean . . .
                and that it would be put in the hands of the
                Papists in the event of his untimely death.
                You left yourself open, Kit.

                (ROSALINDA *stirs.*)

ROSALINDA   Oh go to sleep! Can't you ever sleep?

                (SKERES *creeps off.* ROSALINDA *subsides.*)

MARLOWE   (*gazing at her*) That's what I should write in
          Venice . . . the Venetian story she once told
          us - about the Moorish general and his
          jealousy. A good theme, jealousy. (*He glances
          at* STONE.) She would be Disdemone and I the
          Moor . . . she in white make-up, me in black
          . . . and you could be the damned machiavel
          ensign that dupes him into murdering her!
          They creep up on her in her sleep, hit her with
          a sandbag and pull down the roof on her to
          make it look like misadventure. No . . . too
          much like *The Jew of Malta*.

STONE   I think the Moor should do the murder himself
          . . . alone . . . without Iago.

MARLOWE   Without the mach-ivel? How?

STONE   He kills her for love by kissing her to death
          . . . and smothering her with a pillow.

          (MARLOWE *is taken aback by the way that*
          STONE *has been thinking it out and has the
          answer so complete. It increases his fear of
          impotence.*)

MARLOWE   Well we'll see how you do it.

STONE   But it's yours.

MARLOWE   Yours! I felt it sucked into you the moment
          you spoke of it. I want to see how it develops
          . . . as the critics say . . .

STONE   No . . .

MARLOWE   Yes! Wouldn't surprise me if you've written
          it already . . . in the cracks between making
          love and making excuses for me being unable
          to write a line! Oh yes! You've written *Venus
          and Adonis* in the time it's taken me to get
          through a third of *Leander*! And through it all

streams of sonnets gushing forth! You're like
a gargoyle in a storm!

STONE   It was all stored up in me when I came to
Scadbury. All I needed was regular meals, no
worries about the next day . . . and the right
company.

MARLOWE   They say a whale only swallows you in
swallowing the sea. It means no harm. It does
it smiling.

ROSALINDA   I don't care what happens . . . how we fare or
how we face it . . . but I have to sleep!

MARLOWE   Disdemone! Disdemone! Say your prayers,
I'm going to kiss you to death!

ROSALINDA   *Io ho bisogno di dormire!* [I need to sleep!]

                 (*She avoids him and goes to exit.*)

                 Why is it you never close your eyes?

                 (*Once she's gone* STONE *becomes urgent.*)

STONE   You could slip away. Not go to Deptford with
them. Choose your own route. There's half a
dozen ports you could sail from to the
continent or Venice . . .

MARLOWE   Yes.

STONE   They can put it out that you died at Deptford.
You don't have to be there!

MARLOWE   In the dead man's switch you have to stay
close to the dead man till the last possible
moment or it doesn't work. Have you finished
the copy?

STONE   Yes.

MARLOWE   You might as well finish the poem too. Hardly
            my theme, is it? You can see impatience
            setting in. Leander sees Hero, lusts after her,
            swims the Hellespont and talks his way into
            bed and I'm still not half way! I think I only
            did it because he spends most of the poem
            with his clothes off . . . what did you think?

STONE   I only see a serenity that I could never match.

            (*He finds the place in the manuscript of Hero
            and Leander.*)

            "Thus near the bed she blushing stood
                                              upright,
            And from her countenance behold ye might
            A kind of twilight break, which through the
                                                  hair
            As from an orient cloud, glimps'd here and
                                                 there;
            And round about the chamber this false morn
            Brought forth the day before the day was born."

MARLOWE   She's you. No sooner had we met than you
            had your shirt off. But it was false morn with
            you, too.

STONE   Did Ingram say he'd be at Deptford?

MARLOWE   It wasn't with me . . .

STONE   I think he will. And I think he . . . the three of
            them . . . were the ones who had Kyd arrested.
            When we all laughed about my sword being
            buttoned . . . and Poley talked about Ralegh's
            men using venom on their swords . . . he said:
            "pointed with poison". It's a quotation from
            Kyd's play . . . the one he was writing.
            There's a practice duel between the revenger
            and another who uses an unbuttoned sword
            with poison on it. The play is still being
            written! Poley could only have seen it in
            Kyd's room!

MARLOWE   How did *you* know about the play?

STONE   Kyd talked about it.

MARLOWE   Where? In prison?

             (STONE *sees that* MARLOWE *has guessed.*)

             You've visited him in Bridewell, haven't you?

STONE   He's not your enemy . . .

MARLOWE   What are you trying to do to me?

STONE   He's a broken man. I doubt if he'll last the
             year . . .

MARLOWE   How many deaths d'you want me to die?

STONE   I don't want you to die! Nor does he! He only
             tells them what he thinks they know already!

             (MARLOWE *grabs a sword.*)

MARLOWE   Someone gave you permission to see him.
             That someone would have to be important.
             Did they use you to question him?

STONE   No! I interceded for him!

MARLOWE   Who with?

STONE   One of Robert Cecil's men. I can't name him.

MARLOWE   Is he the one that pays you?

             (*A pause.* STONE *decides to tell.*)

STONE   Yes.

MARLOWE   He puts the money in your hand?

STONE   Yes!

MARLOWE   Who does it come from?

STONE   The Queen!

MARLOWE   So that's whose man you are! Hers! What are
               your orders?

STONE   To watch over your safety! I'm here to help
               you! I was told that the Queen was concerned
               for your safety. I was to report any danger . . .
               and now I see danger I daren't leave you to
               report it.

MARLOWE   Dear Touch. You're deceived. Her only
               concern is whether I should be killed for
               sodomy, atheism or treason . . . and which
               dreadful deaths to devise. Perhaps, for
               sodomy, the one they used on Edward the
               Second that I was not allowed to put in the
               play. Held down while a cow's horn was
               inserted in his anus and a red hot iron pushed
               through to his bowels. No, that was a secret
               killing arranged so that when the horn was
               taken out there was no mark visible on the
               body. They wouldn't want that! What use is
               an invisible injury to the state? Well, it'll just
               have to be the genitals sewn in the mouth, the
               body unjointed, immersed in the Thames,
               beheaded, quartered, dragged through the
               streets by swine and finally . . . unless
               someone has a fit of inspiration . . . set fire
               to. Don't you think it would have been better
               if we'd been lovers?

               (STONE *reaches out falteringly to touch him.*)

STONE   Yes. If it could have been possible. Yes, I
               think so with all my heart.

MARLOWE   He wouldn't let you though, would he? The
               one you carry on your back? When you first
               came I felt you were like some other self . . .
               some reflection of me. I thought I was no

longer alone. But behind the reflection swam the whale!

STONE   You know why I came . . .

MARLOWE   To swallow me!

STONE   To help! I came to help you!

MARLOWE   Help? What help? How can the whale help Jonah when Jonah's inside the whale?

             (*The noise of their shouting rouses first* ROSALINDA *then the other two.*)

ROSALINDA   What's happened?

             (MARLOWE *looks in terror at* STONE.)

MARLOWE   I'm in his belly! Make him spew me up!

             (ROSALINDA *embraces* MARLOWE *like embracing a frightened child.*)

STONE   I want to help . . .

ROSALINDA   Keep away!

             (SKERES *and* POLEY *have entered.*)

POLEY   Now, now Christopher!

             (SKERES *and* POLEY *are not unused to this kind of thing from him.*)

SKERES   What have you been doing?

POLEY   Breakfast. That's what you need.

ROSALINDA   (*points at* STONE) Get him away!

SKERES   Oh my head! (*Holds his head.*) Christ!

POLEY   Come on friend. Help us get on the road.
               We'll have our eggs at the Moon and Stars.

               (SKERES *and* POLEY *take* STONE *off*.)

ROSALINDA   I loathe him! They can do what they like to
               him!

MARLOWE   The papers! The School of Night papers . . . I
               want you to get them . . .

ROSALINDA   Where from?

MARLOWE   They're at Scadbury. They've been there all
               the time. I can't go there. You can.

ROSALINDA   Where do I look?

MARLOWE   Bound in the covers of a book. My *Principles
               of Alchemy*.

ROSALINDA   So they were there . . . under Ralegh's nose . . .

MARLOWE   (*giving letter*) This tells you where to take
               them. (*Indicates off stage*.) Put it away! Don't
               tell Touch . . . but let him help you in any
               other way.

ROSALINDA   No!

MARLOWE   Yes!

ROSALINDA   But he's spoiled everything!

MARLOWE   You can't blame the whale for swallowing.

               (*Enter* STONE, SKERES *and* POLEY *in
               background*.)

STONE   We're ready.

MARLOWE   (*indicates* ROSALINDA) Touch . . . you said you
               could hide her . . . (*He hands his dagger to
               him*.) Look after her. Guard her.

ROSALINDA   But I'm coming to Deptford!

MARLOWE   No.

ROSALINDA   I must!

MARLOWE   Too dangerous . . .

POLEY   He's right Princess. Three's enough.

                 (ROSALINDA *accepts that he must go alone.*)

ROSALINDA   The house! You know nothing . . . If it's
                 locked there's a boatman called Guido who
                 keeps the keys. And take the room with the
                 crimson curtains. You'll know why when you
                 stand at the window.

STONE   (*quietly to* MARLOWE) I can't let you go . . .

MARLOWE   You already have. Didn't you feel it? "The
                 Lord spake unto the whale and it did vomit up
                 Jonah, on to the dry land."

                 (MARLOWE *moves away, pausing to touch*
                 ROSALINDA's *face. The lights fade.*)

                              Scene Five

*The room at Deptford . . . lit first as before, then with a look
of stark reality . . . even though every detail is the same as
the room in* MARLOWE's *imagination.*

FRIZER, POLEY *and* SKERES *stand with their backs to* MARLOWE
who faces the audience.

MARLOWE   An upper room overlooking the Thames at
                 Deptford Strand. And, I could swear, the same
                 room! Three figures. The same smell of
                 water. Except that this is real. No more
                 Alchemist's visions. And no more Dog.
                 Somewhere along the way he left me. To pad

the Dog-path to the skies, watched over by
His own Dog Star. Or did he drift down the
river as so many do . . . Down from the Isle of
Dogs, mourned by Dogfish, to the Dogger
Bank . . . and thence in a cloud of sea spray
to the deep? Amen to Dog. And amen all false
dreams. Yes! I feel curiously free . . .

(*He turns as do the three men. On the table is
a laced-up sack containing the corpse.* SKERES
begins to unlace it.)

Why Ingram! We weren't expecting you!

FRIZER   I've been talking to Danby, the coroner.
There's a problem. We were told the corpse
was unmarked - that he'd choked to death on
his own vomit so we could pass him off as
having drowned. We were cheated. As you see
. . . he was stabbed in the eye. Take a look.

(MARLOWE, *reluctant, moves nearer.*)

POLEY   Straight through the top of the right lid. It's a
good inch wide.

FRIZER   Danby won't have it covered or disguised. He
thinks it too risky. Sixteen jurors at the
inquest. They mightn't know Kit Marlowe
from Adam but it's a fair assumption that one
or two will know a knife wound when they
see one.

MARLOWE   So how do we say I died?

POLEY   Knifed?

FRIZER   It's what Danby insists on us saying that
counts. He's going to report the eye wound as
the cause of death. (*To* POLEY.) Take it . . .

SKERES   Kit!

(He waves the dead man's hand at him. Then
POLEY *and* SKERES *manhandle the corpse just*
out of sight in an adjoining room.)

MARLOWE   "Stabbed by person unknown"?

FRIZER   He won't agree to that either. It would mean a
           search . . . a hue and cry. He wants an open
           and shut case.

MARLOWE   What will he agree too?

FRIZER   If we claimed one of us did it accidentally in
           a bit of horse play it would look like a cover
           up. Danby wants us to say that you started a
           fight and that one of us was forced to kill you
           in self-defence.

           *(*MARLOWE *had begun to suspect this.)*

MARLOWE   Who's to do it?

FRIZER   Me.

           *(*POLEY *has returned.)*

POLEY   He's got the cleanest record.

MARLOWE   You won't escape prison.

FRIZER   No. But three months at the most, to put a
           good face on it. Then acquittal. Self-defence.

MARLOWE   Will she guarantee the pardon?

SKERES   Oh Kit! This is cast iron. They won't want
           revealed what goes on here.

MARLOWE   *(to* FRIZER*)* But why would you do such a
           thing for me?

FRIZER   Everyone is co-operating to one end . . . your
           safe passage out of this country.

(MARLOWE *gives him a disbelieving look.*)

Sit on the bed.

(MARLOWE *sits on the trestle bed downstage.*)

You two sit at the table with me.

MARLOWE   This stinks of semen. Or should I say sailors?

(FRIZER *takes out a set of dice.*)

FRIZER   This is what I've agreed with Danby. We are
              rolling dice. You pick a quarrel with me . . . a
              dispute about the bill for the meal and drinks
              and so on. Tempers roused. You draw your
              dagger.

(MARLOWE *grins.*)

MARLOWE   Shakespear has it.

POLEY   Take mine . . .

FRIZER   No. The blade's too thick for the cut.

(SKERES *shows his.* FRIZER *examines it.*)

              So's yours.

POLEY   Must have been stabbed with a skewer. Give
              him yours.

FRIZER   It's inscribed . . .

SKERES   Name on your knife! Never!

FRIZER   No matter. We'll say you took it off me. Out
              of my belt. Take it from me. Come up behind.

POLEY   Good! I've seen that happen thousands of
              times . . .

(MARLOWE *takes the knife.*)

FRIZER   You go to wound me. I grab your wrist. In the
                struggle to defend myself I turn the knife . . .
                etcetera . . .

SKERES   What do we do?

FRIZER   Get the story straight and don't wander off it.

                (FRIZER *noses around, checking.*)

                His clothes?

                (POLEY *holds up a bundle of* MARLOWE'S
                clothes.)

                What's the ship?

SKERES   The Easterling. Ready on the tide. We'll take
                you aboard at the last moment.

FRIZER   *I'll* take him aboard. Did you walk him in the
                garden?

SKERES   Yes.

FRIZER   You made sure he was seen.

SKERES   We did.

FRIZER   Who by?

                (POLEY *points downstairs.*)

POLEY   Old Elly. Madam Tits. She saw him. I called
                her to the window. I named him. I said: "This
                is Master Marlowe" . . . and he kept his face
                turned away. She'll testify she saw him
                walking.

SKERES   But we never let her see him too close. She'll
                identify the corpse as his, no fear.

POLEY   (*to* SKERES) Stanislaus. Let's dress him.

(*He nods towards the corpse. They exit to the next room.*)

MARLOWE   Albeit you've set this up to effect my escape there are some who might look at it shrewdly and think the plan would serve just as well if you intended murder. The highest coroner in the land has been primed to pronounce, in the next few days that a certain corpse has been killed in self-defence . . . by you. Whichever corpse he happens to find on his table. Danby has no idea what I look like. The detail's good, too. I'm well known for picking quarrels . . . and drawing knives!

(*He moves quickly behind* FRIZER *and puts the knife to his throat.*)

Nick! Robyn! Where I can see you!

(*They enter.*)

I'm not Tom Kyd!

(FRIZER *indicates with a look. They keep back.*)

What did he really die of, our Polack? Whose was the last face he saw on earth? I'll say it again: I am not Tom Kyd! I'm a writer of the head . . . not the heart. Nick. You and I owe each other something . . . don't we?

SKERES   Yes, Kit.

MARLOWE   Is this a plan to kill me?

SKERES   No. If it is it's news to me.

MARLOWE   Swear by God.

SKERES   You don't believe in Him.

MARLOWE   No. But you do.

SKERES   Then by Almighty God . . .

MARLOWE   Say it! It's not a plan to kill me . . .

SKERES   It's not a plan to kill you.

MARLOWE   Danger sharpens me, Ingram; you should
               know that. I'm no longer "Hithercorpse".

POLEY   Leave him. Get on board. We won't follow.

MARLOWE   You're not killing me off. (*Thinks of* STONE.)
               And nor is he . . .

POLEY   Who's this?

MARLOWE   The one Ingram brought to Scadbury . . .

FRIZER   I'd never seen him before!

MARLOWE   Dear Touch. Sweet William. You can hold up
               your mirror and amaze the world. But you
               couldn't write the play I have in mind. Get
               me a theatre . . . just for one afternoon . . .
               and it'll all be said. And not in code or
               cipher. That's their game. Out front. We'll
               start a School of Day! They steal our light
               and call it God's or Gloriana's . . . We'll take
               it back and call it Truth!

               (*He teases* FRIZER *with the knife.*)

               And do you think you could kill that Ingram?
               He does! He really does! That's what you're
               here for, isn't it?

               (FRIZER *spins about and grabs his wrist.* KIT
               regards him with contempt.)

               You think a rat like you could blot out the
               sun?

               (FRIZER *appears to thrust the knife into*
               MARLOWE'S *right eye. He screams.* SKERES *and*
               POLEY *rush to catch him.*)

SKERES   Take it out! Take the knife out!

POLEY   It's out! Staunch it!

               (SKERES *gets a cloth.* FRIZER *is still, staring at
               the knife.* MARLOWE *dies.*)

SKERES   (*to* FRIZER) May you be damned!

               (*Blackout.*)

Scene Six

A stage almost bare for St. Nicholas' churchyard, Deptford.

Before the scene is lit we hear STONE'S VOICE *reading from
the coroner's report.*

STONE'S   A certain Ingram Frizer, late of London, and
VOICE   the aforesaid Christopher Marlowe and one
               Nicholas Skeres and Robert Poley, on the
               thirtieth day of May, at Deptford Strand,
               within the verge, about the tenth hour before
               noon of the same day, met together in a room
               in the house of a certain Eleanor Bull, widow,
               and there passed the time together . . .

               (*The lights rise to reveal* STONE *and*
               ROSALINDA, *the latter dressed in a boat cloak
               and hood for her journey to Venice.* STONE
               reads from a paper.)

               It so befell that the said Christopher Marlowe
               on a sudden and of his malice towards the
               said Ingram aforethought, was at his back,
               whereupon the said Ingram, in defence of his
               life, with the dagger aforesaid of the value of
               twelve pence, gave the said Christopher a
               mortal wound over his right eye of the depth
               of two inches and the width of one inch; of
               which aforesaid wound the aforesaid

Christopher Marlowe then and there instantly
died.

ROSALINDA   He's there. In Venice. In my home. He could
be in my very room, looking out on the water.

(STONE *indicates a grave.*)

STONE   By my calculations this has to be the grave.
It's the only unmarked one, freshly dug.

ROSALINDA   But he's not in it!

STONE   I beg you out of all the love I have for you
just to consider that it could be possible.

ROSALINDA   I shall see him in Venice. That's what's
possible.

STONE   Just give us time to find out if he's arrived.

ROSALINDA   You want me to believe him dead because
that's what you want to believe!

STONE   No!

ROSALINDA   He was afraid of no one except you . . . But
now he has his room by the water he'll sail
far beyond you!

STONE   Don't make me out his enemy . . . or yours. I
loved him! I love you!

ROSALINDA   A writer's words, spoken by an actor. I'm
going to him.

STONE   What can he offer you?

ROSALINDA   You don't see, do you, the bond he has with
me . . . and I with him? He was born low and
raised himself high. The shepherd boy became
Tamburlaine! He raised me! He took me to a
high place and showed me the world. But in
the end I could only see him. As fast as he

broke the chains I had in here (*Her mind.*) he
bound me to him. He has made enemies of all
who love him - except one. And she will
never break faith.

(*She exits.* STONE *watches her go and, as he
does so, hears a man whistling. An* OFFICER OF
THE WATCH *enters, heavily armed. He regards*
STONE *with a keen suspicion.*)

OFFICER   Good day, sir. Officer of the Watch, sir.

STONE   Good day . . . Who do you watch? The dead?

OFFICER   And the living, sir. Were you looking for a
            particular grave?

            (STONE *calms himself.*)

STONE   No. Just passing through.

OFFICER   Not always easy to know who's who, sir . . .
            not when there's no stone.

            (STONE *realises that this man is not there by
            chance.*)

STONE   That's true . . .

OFFICER   Reverend'll be very pleased . . . you taking an
            interest in an unmarked grave. He'll say a
            prayer for him . . . whoever he is. Who shall I
            say inquired?

            (STONE *gives him a warning look, as though
            saying: "touch me not."*)

STONE   A gentleman.

            (*The* OFFICER, *outfaced, moves away and exits.*
            STONE *turns to contemplate the grave.*)

            The lights fade.